Teacher Shortages and the Challenge of Retention

Teacher Shortages and the Challenge of Retention

Practices That Make School Systems and Cultures More Attractive and Empowering

Barbara J. Smith

ROWMAN & LITTLEFIELD
Lanham • Boulder • New York • London

Published by Rowman & Littlefield
An imprint of The Rowman & Littlefield Publishing Group, Inc.
4501 Forbes Boulevard, Suite 200, Lanham, Maryland 20706
www.rowman.com

86-90 Paul Street, London EC2A 4NE, United Kingdom

Copyright © 2023 by Barbara J. Smith

All rights reserved. No part of this book may be reproduced in any form or by any electronic or mechanical means, including information storage and retrieval systems, without written permission from the publisher, except by a reviewer who may quote passages in a review.

British Library Cataloguing in Publication Information Available

Library of Congress Cataloging-in-Publication Data

Names: Smith, Barbara J., 1956– author.
Title: Teacher shortages and the challenge of retention : practices that make school systems and cultures more attractive and empowering / Barbara J. Smith.
Description: Lanham, Maryland: Rowman & Littlefield, 2023. | Includes bibliographical references. | Summary: "Teacher Shortage and the Challenge of Retention was written to address the need to transform many teaching conditions in schools today"— Provided by publisher.
Identifiers: LCCN 2023001348 (print) | LCCN 2023001349 (ebook) | ISBN 9781475870824 (cloth) | ISBN 9781475870831 (paperback) | ISBN 9781475870848 (epub)
Subjects: LCSH: Teachers—Recruiting—United States. | Teacher turnover—United States—Prevention. | School environment—United States.
Classification: LCC LB2835.25 .S65 2023 (print) | LCC LB2835.25 (ebook) | DDC 371.14—dc23/eng/20230203
LC record available at https://lccn.loc.gov/2023001348
LC ebook record available at https://lccn.loc.gov/2023001349

*To Willy Timmermans,
my high school music teacher
who found a way to make everyone
musical and appreciate the joy of creativity
that comes from an inspired teacher.*

Contents

Foreword	ix
Acknowledgments	xiii
Introduction: Changing the Landscape of Teaching	xv
Chapter 1: Pay Day	1
Chapter 2: Significantly Reducing Class Size	7
Chapter 3: Time to Polish, Prepare, and Reflect	11
Chapter 4: Time to Teach and Learn	21
Chapter 5: Time for Robust Professional Learning	27
Chapter 6: Reducing the Volume of Expectations	37
Chapter 7: Trusting Teachers' Capacities to Assess Students	49
Chapter 8: Respect and Recognition of Teacher Insight, Action, and Creativity	55
Chapter 9: Teaching Supports	61
Chapter 10: Meaningful Mentorship Support and Performance Appraisal	67
Chapter 11: Family Communication and Interaction	75
Chapter 12: Ample Access to Resources	81
Chapter 13: Stunning and Stimulating Spaces	91
Chapter 14: Teacher Leadership Opportunities	95
Chapter 15: Health and Safety	103

Conclusion: I Want to Be a Teacher 107
Bibliography 113
About the Author 119

Foreword

Imagine that you are walking past a school and you notice smoke billowing from the roof and flames shooting out the windows. You hear the cries of children and teachers trying to escape the danger. Here are your choices:

1. Commission a study to learn about the impact of fires on schools.
2. Engage a strategic consulting firm to create a five-year plan in the event of fire.
3. Conduct a focus group to determine whether there is sufficient buy-in to take action in the event of fire.
4. Run to the building and evacuate the children and teachers who are facing mortal peril.

In the compelling evidence and arguments that Barbara Smith has laid out in the pages that follow, the author systematically decimates the arguments and excuses that prefer the status quo, ignore the impending global crisis resulting from the teacher shortage, and insists that we stop temporizing and start taking decisive action. The future of our profession and, most importantly, the future of our students depend on it.

Smith provides the reader with some challenging insights that will not be universally popular but are vitally necessary. This is why policymakers, union leaders, administrators, classroom teachers and, most importantly, citizens who vote for governing boards and legislators must take seriously these challenging ideas.

First, money is necessary but not sufficient. It does not require a randomized control trial study to conclude that a five-figure income does not sustain six-figure debt. But as the alarming rate of teacher turnover—especially in high-poverty and rural schools—indicates, money alone is not sufficient to stem the tide of teachers leaving our profession. The common refrains that I hear from teachers who are retiring early, transferring to less stressful positions in education, or leaving the profession entirely are that they require not only fair compensation but respect, safety, professional autonomy, collaboration, and learning. The staff shortages, including not only teachers but also substitute teachers and paraprofessionals, lead to exhaustion and burnout and undermine the time needed for lesson planning, collaboration, and professional learning. As Smith has noted, the educational world is fortunate indeed to have dedicated professionals who will, without exaggeration, work themselves to death in the service of students. But heroism is not a sustainable strategy. If there is a future to public education, it cannot depend upon ever greater sacrifices of time, family, and health that too many teachers have made.

Second, the solution to the teacher shortage depends on effective educational leadership. The Gallup organization's research on engagement makes clear that people do not quit jobs. They quit managers. In the realm of education, we know that teacher effectiveness has the greatest impact on student achievement, but we sometimes fail to recognize that the greatest impact of retaining great teachers lands on effective educational leaders. These are the people who not only observe and evaluate classroom teachers but jump into the fray to take over a class to give teachers the time to collaborate and learn from one another. These are the leaders who leave the demands of policymakers to evaluate teachers with the leadership imperatives of encouragement, nurturing, and support. We cannot address the teacher shortage without simultaneously addressing the need for effective leadership at every level.

Third, civil discourse is a democratic imperative. Vigorous debate is part of that discourse, but the recent trends that vilify and threaten teachers make their jobs untenable. Most pernicious are the anonymous tip lines that some jurisdictions have adopted that encourage students to report teachers who fail to adhere strictly to the curriculum demands. Reasonable people can differ about curriculum, whether it is on the relative weight to place on geometry or statistics, the most effective way to teach literacy skills to primary students, or the best way to teach critical thinking in social studies and science. But these discussions cross the boundary of civil discourse when disagreements turn into threats not only to teachers but to their families. Teachers in Australia, the United Kingdom, and the United States invest enormous intellectual energy in placing the history of those nations in the context of 21st-century racial inequities. That is not, to put a fine point on it, critical race theory, nor is it indoctrination of young malleable minds. Our job as teachers is to create space for inquiry, deliberation, debate, and deep understanding. We can lead our students in pledging allegiance to the flag or singing "God Save the King" and nevertheless help them understand that valuing the freedoms they enjoy today were not without enormous sacrifices by people less privileged than our students. To prepare our students for the world of postsecondary education, work, and, most broadly, their roles as citizens requires that we fearlessly entertain ideas that are different from our own. At the very least, our students need to see that adults and students can disagree with one another and still be friends. That is a quality sadly missing from much of the discourse our students see from the adults who dominate the airwaves and internet.

Fourth, teachers deserve and demand respect. When I was a teacher in China decades ago, teachers made the equivalent of $35 per month and lived eight to a room in bunk beds. But when we walked down the street, we were invariably greeted with respect. The profession of teaching was not dissimilar to officers in the military or clergy in the American South. While none of those professions were remunerative, they were all rewarded with well-earned respect. I'm not unaware of the political differences that many readers may have with the Chinese regime, but my teacher friends there know that friendship has no borders and that, despite differences in policy, we can nevertheless learn much from one another when it comes to valuing the professional educator. I am not suggesting that teachers are without flaws—I know that I am not. But I am suggesting that the operating presumption in too many conversations with parents is that the teacher is wrong and the student is right. I always wonder if the parents who propagate this point of view plan to move into the college dorms with their children and accompany them to their first job. At some point students need to accept and respect feedback, apply that feedback, and improve their performance. School is a good place to practice that essential life skill.

Fifth, we need decisive steps to make the professions of teaching and educational leadership more family friendly. A common stereotype is that teachers work from 7:30 a.m. to 3:00 p.m., enjoy summers off, and have loads of time for leisure. The time stamps on the emails I receive from teachers around the world tell a different story. They are inundated with texts and emails and accompanying demands for immediate responses. They are turned into data entry clerks thanks to the growing number of computerized grading systems that list dozens of academic content standards that teachers are expected to evaluate. When the demands of teaching and leadership become time-consuming infringements on family time, then we have required that these professionals choose between career and family. The responsibilities of child care and elder care, especially during the global pandemic, have fallen disproportionately on women. No matter how dedicated they may be to their profession, the family sacrifices that are required of teachers and administrators are too great to bear for our colleagues now in the profession, making these jobs unattractive to those promising future educators who refuse to sacrifice family and health for a career.

This is a book not merely to be read but to be studied. The "Challenge Chats" that Dr. Smith provides present an ideal focus for a rich discussion that will take these vital ideas from theory to reality. While the intended audience includes practitioners, leaders, and policymakers, I hope that parents, students, and community members who value public education and the future of our children will also engage in these conversations.

While these pages offer glimpses of a positive and hopeful future, the global education community must be mindful of what the future looks like if we fail to follow Smith's advice. That is a world of increasing inequities in which the failure of policies to restore educational professionals will have multidecade consequences. When the system fails teachers, the students, their families, and their communities pay the price. The staggering cost of educational failures includes lifetimes of unemployment, poverty, health care needs, and criminal justice system involvement. If anyone thinks that Smith's prescriptions are too costly, they should consider the far greater cost that all of us will pay if we fail to heed her warnings.

Douglas Reeves
Chief Executive Officer, Creative Leadership Solutions
Boston, Massachusetts USA

Acknowledgments

I am thankful that writing has never been an isolated experience for me. I believe my first taste of putting word to print—beyond the stuff submitted for grading—was the invitation to submit poems for the school yearbook and then, years later, in my first year of teaching in curriculum design groups supported by the Waterloo County Board of Education. After a few decades, making my way to be a more seasoned educator, I was asked to work on a project with Jackie Copp to cowrite *Mining for Gems,* a summary of best practices in independent schools in Canada. To the members of the Sarnia Central High School yearbook selection committee; my supervisor, Wayne Somerville in Waterloo; and Jackie and the team at the Canadian Accredited Independent Schools (CAIS), I am truly grateful for these opportunities that did sow such early writing seeds.

These initial pen-to-paper experiences coupled with being an educator in public, independent, charter, and international schools from K through graduate schools cultivated a confidence and desire to share ideas. It took a year to write *A Charter School Principal Story*, but it could not have happened without the support of the staff, particularly those who were open to new approaches and trusted outlier ideas: Mr. Carter, Ms. Nugent Chang, Ms. Cherry, Mr. Dickens, Ms. Miles Cordova, Dr. Ginsburg, Ms. Johnson, Ms. Kensler, Ms. LeVault, Ms. Almonte Lopez, Mr. McKeiver, Ms. Narrow, Ms. Robbins, Ms. Robinson, Mr. Sessoms, Ms. Palmer, and Ms. Vernaiz. Working with such champions was truly inspiring.

There are a host of educators, school leaders, and passionate community members who have made considerable impressions, all informing and influencing my voice. These include the following: Madeleine Allan, David Booth, Susana Calley, Mike Carter, Denise Cherry, Bob Chilton, Jim Christopher, Luke Coles, Josh Cooper, Mike Crowley, Radu Elias, Rosemary Evans, Don Fawcett, Lisa Gonzales, Craig Griffie, Mhairi Johnson, Dennis Kellison, Diane Manica, Susan McGroddy, Jack Miller, Shaune Palmer, Martha Perry, Skip Phoenix, Angela Purcell, Valerie Rixon, Ian Robinson, Jalen Rose,

Michelle Ruscitti-Miller, Keith Russell, Anne Shaw, Dave Stevenson, Brian Stone, Michael Thompson, Valerie Turner, Tony Upson, Emily Walton-Doris, William Williams, Lauren Black Willms, Anne Wintemute, Kirk Wipper, and Rick Wormeli.

More recently, working with the editorial team at Rowman & Littlefield has been so fulfilling. Tom Koerner, Kira Hall, and Carlie Wall have been instrumental and inspirational in moving *How Much Does a Great School Cost: School Economies and School Values*, *Assessment Tools and Systems* and, now, *Teacher Shortages and the Challenge of Retention* to fruition. Finding a publisher fit for a writer is not easy when you are sharing schooling ideas that color outside the lines. I truly appreciate their trust and willingness to stretch educational boundaries with me.

There are a host of reviewers of my work that contribute often by sharing feedback, endorsements, and letting their networks know about this book. Way before this work became a published text, a manuscript was polished by many experts who gave their time generously to help bring this project to completion. I am truly thankful for the support and input from Hope Blecher, Liam Exelby, Kathleen Fox, Beverly Freedman, Bena Kallick, Michael Lawrence, Brandon Oddo, John Neretlis, Douglas Reeves, and Elliott Seif.

My family and friends are my rocks. They tolerate my ongoing escapes to the laptop, and they smile politely when I exceed my elevator speech promoting the merits and limitations of the teaching profession. They know firsthand that being a teacher is a serious commitment of time and that doing things the same way won't solve any problems today or tomorrow. To Simon, Sarah, Martin, Molly, and an incredible mix of lifelong friends, I thank you all for understanding the education part of me that just won't quit.

Introduction
Changing the Landscape of Teaching

> *Walt wanted his park to be different in that it would lack the dirtiness and deterioration that was typically present at amusement parks.*[1]
>
> —Reece Fischer

It took years for Walt Disney to turn around the perception that a carnival could be a clean, family-focused, entertainment-theme-park destination. Much like Disney changed the face of what amusement parks could be, schools and school systems must consider building new foundations to meet the growing needs of students, teachers, and society.

A new landscape for teaching could mean many changes, including a significant and sustainable response to the calls for smaller class sizes and quality time for planning. By looking outside the fixed walls of schooling, it is possible to restructure schools to make working and learning conditions much more appealing and effective for all students and teachers.

Disney's transformational vision did not happen overnight; it was a constant trial and error with many reconfigurations along the way. It could take years for the culture of education to implement significant changes that could impact the teaching topography and practice of schooling. The only problem is, we do not have years.

Lasting change should not take a decade to implement; it simply loses steam along the way, making the more comfortable path back to the past ways of doing things seem more tolerable and doable. The good news is there are plenty of talented educators who have the capacity to make inspiring changes happen in schools.

Teacher Shortages and the Challenge of Retention is about moving forward while reaching back to a time when teachers felt empowered, engaged, and fulfilled in their profession, a time when the demand to enter teacher college was much higher than occupiable spaces in many schools of education.

In 1980, after applying to over 100 school districts, I received only two interviews. This is no longer the case. Anya Kamenetz (2022) points out that, according to the Bureau of Labor Statistics in the United States, "there are 567,000 fewer educators in America's public schools today than there were before the pandemic. And the NEA's (National Education Association) analysis of BLS data indicates that 43% of jobs posted are going unfilled."[2]

The problem of teacher retention is an issue across many global regions. According to a survey conducted by the National Education Union in the UK, "nearly half of teachers in England plan to quit within the next five years . . . 44% of teachers plan to leave the profession by 2027, a fifth (22%) said they would leave within two years."[3] Pasi Sahlberg (2022) indicated that more than a third of early career Australian teachers are quitting the profession within their first five years. He added, "Most of these qualified teachers start excited and depart exhausted."[4]

To transform schools, the current organizational structure as well as the systems and operations that implement what stakeholders experience as schooling would need to change. For such change to take hold, teachers need to be at the core of generating, implementing, and adapting a new forward in education.

This book shares ideas about what such changes could be like, how change could benefit teachers and students alike, and how it could influence a positive shift in society. Before addressing significant reforms in teacher practice, it's important to outline what kinds of experiences make the teaching profession attractive to some and not to others. Taking a closer look at teacher's stories—what drives them to stay and leave, what makes them feel empowered or not, and what makes them feel fulfilled in the role—is this starting point for further exploration.

Without taking the time to unravel the complexities of the profession, many may assume that teachers are people who enjoy working with children and making a difference in their lives. While some teachers may be drawn to the summers off or the winter and spring breaks, it is doubtful that such shallow incentives propel most individuals to the profession. Depending on the job, some potential educators may be attracted to the prospect, over time, of earning a six-digit salary, but studies have found that pay alone is not what brings people to the profession.

The downsides to a career in education, however, need to be addressed with the goal of creating new options for those who take on such important roles in society. By identifying the obstacles, it is possible to generate new contexts for practice, which can not only limit the challenges but create conditions for teachers and students to thrive.

It is difficult to attract teacher talent when the following are true:

Introduction

xvii

- Salaries tend to be less than other professions.
- There are too many students in classrooms.
- There is not enough time to polish, prepare and reflect.
- School schedules do not provide enough time for most students to master learning.
- Meaningful, ongoing professional learning is not provided.
- There is too much curriculum to teach.
- There is a lack of trust in teacher's capacity to assess students.
- Teacher insight, action and creativity is not respected and rarely recognized.
- Teacher supports are limited.
- There are few teacher-leaders available to mentor new teachers in a school.
- Performance appraisals are disconnected from professional learning.
- Time to interact with families is limited.
- Access to classroom resources are limited.
- The workplace setting may be tired and uninspiring.
- Opportunities for upward mobility are limited.
- There is reduced leadership support when supervisors have too many direct reports.
- Health and wellness of community members is lacking.
- Safe working conditions cannot be guaranteed.

Considering such a lengthy list of the drawbacks, it is astounding that there are so many dedicated professionals remaining in the field. Nevertheless, just because there are teachers assigned to classes today, this doesn't mean that anyone should assume they will always be there or that we will attract quality candidates to all teacher-preparation institutions. The good news is that many schooling systems can be rewired to reduce or eliminate such shortcomings.

This book calls for widescale change, the kind that synthesizes and encourages improved and informed practices, the kind that makes teachers and students engaged, empowered, and inspired to go to school. This book is not about going back to school in the sense of going back to past habits of operation. Rather, it's about coming back to a future school in heart and mind with the autonomy, trust, and capacity to build better institutions for learning. Even though there are passionate teachers in today's schools, many have left the building.

What would turn tired schools into resorts of the innovative and imaginative kind? What can be done to rekindle a teacher's fire and passion? What can administrators do to support teachers? What can trustees and parents do to be better informed about current educational research? What role can community members play in supporting school change?

This book is organized into chapters that coincide with concrete ways of addressing specific challenges that face many educators and school systems every day.

Chapter 1 opens with a focus on "Pay Day" and the underlying question, Do we really pay teachers what they deserve? The reality that a college degree tends to bring higher wages and benefits to those who do not choose a teaching career is a serious deterrent that can influence interest and talent adversely. In this day and age, teachers who have demonstrated expertise in their craft should be making six-digit salaries, and with this, afforded respectable benefits. Their pay should be commensurate with the role they play in society, now and in the future.

"Significantly Reducing Class Size" is the focus for chapter 2. The inherent need of teachers to reach all their students is at the heart of this chapter that puts forth a coherent argument justifying fewer students in classrooms. Teachers can feel much more fulfilled when they can work in supportive conditions—namely, a formula for class size that maximizes the potential for student learning.

In chapter 3, the idea that teaching is instruction with a few breaks sprinkled throughout the week is put to rest. Teachers need "Time to Polish, Prepare, and Reflect" on their practice if they are going to be engaged in a passionate, continuous pursuit of excellence. Fresh ideas for scheduling and calendar year options are presented for further discussion.

"Time to Teach and Learn" in chapter 4, addresses the need for schools to restructure so there is time for students to experience ideal and informed teaching practices, such as deep learning, inquiry, peer teaching, and learning buddies. Most school schedules do not provide enough time for all students to master learning. School leaders who reach beyond the templates of current school structures can make systematic changes that can make a difference in teaching and learning.

Chapter 5 explains the need for robust professional learning opportunities. This chapter reveals the interconnectedness of quality feedback and performance review that should go hand in hand with invigorating professional growth.

In the next chapter, the recommendation is loud and clear. Schools and school systems must be "Reducing the Volume of Expectations" if there is any hope of building a teaching and learning culture that is sustainable and effective. Like everything else in education, curriculum must evolve and improve over time. Schools that provide interdisciplinary project work and elective options enable current and new knowledge to penetrate the basics; without a link to the real world, learning is distant and disconnected from the learner. By reducing the volume of content in traditional disciplines, it is possible to build a progressive curriculum that leaves room for more authentic engagement.

Chapter 7 focuses on the need for the higher ups to trust teachers to assess students. The overreliance on standardized tests and commercial assessments diminishes the status of the teacher perspective, the person who knows more about what the student understands than anyone. Assessment should be about what students know and should be synthesized, not prioritized over, the process of teaching and learning. Teachers who are trusted to develop diagnostic tests and tests for mastery rather than ranking have much to contribute to building a more effective and meaningful education.

"Respect and Recognition of Teacher Insight, Action, and Creativity," in chapter 8, speaks to the need for schools and school systems to not only value teacher input but encourage creative action. If students are to solve tomorrow's world problems, then they require teacher role models who do the same.

New and more targeted ways of providing "Teacher Supports" is the focus of chapter 9. There exists a smattering of good ideas within so many smorgasbords of offerings (often so many that it can be difficult to consider new options). The need not only for coordinated teacher supports but innovative and meaningful experiences is leveraged with a fresh view of what human supports can be available to help sustain and engage today's teaching force.

Chapter 10 introduces innovative ideas to support "Meaningful Mentorship and Performance Appraisal." The development of an apprenticeship culture with feedback and performance reviews integrated within a cycle of feedback and professional growth is fundamental for a highly evolving and maturing profession. A reduction in the number of direct reports that a supervisor supports and manages is paramount to building progressive and fulfilling teaching cultures.

Chapter 11 addresses the significance of "Family Communication and Interaction." Schools can do much more than go through the typical parent–school interaction motions. Building relationships with parents, like students, is about making meaningful memories. Ideas from innovative schools are shared for purposes of comparison and inspiration. Rather than see parents as necessary obstacles, there are other proactive approaches that can be more supportive for teachers.

Teachers also need ample resources, the highlighted focus in chapter 12. Funds for access to expert ideas, reading materials, and technology must be in alignment with the teacher's needs and the needs of the school. Navigating resource needs can be a challenge, and learning about the breadth of educational materials can be overwhelming. In addition to sharing samples of exceptional resources, this chapter provides a lens or tool that can help distinguish potential assets from dust collectors.

How can teachers feel excited about going to a building every day that is tired and run down? Chapter 13 addresses the need for all schools to be "Stunning and Stimulating Spaces." Novel ideas for shifting the milieu of the entrance, halls, and walls are introduced as prompts for moving away from the image of the crumbling red schoolhouses. Schools can be designed with learning and engagement in mind.

Chapter 14 changes gears to highlight the importance of expanding "Teacher Leadership Opportunities." Studies clearly point out that when teachers have added responsibility, they are more engaged and their students learn more. Innovative ways for restructuring schools "crawling" with leaders are proposed for discussion and consideration.

"Health & Safety" is featured in chapter 15. Teachers must believe their physical and mental well-being are priorities for their employers. Safe working spaces are much more than the installation of metal detectors. Schools can promote healthy teachers in many ways, including the provision of fitness memberships, additional healthcare, insurance, and innovative ideas such as volunteer service days. Health and safety must matter if schools are serious about retaining a thriving teacher population.

The final chapter "I Want to Be a Teacher" proposes that the creation of a culture that fulfills teachers and attracts teaching talent does not lie within one chapter of ideas. It requires the hard work of synthesizing as many needs as possible. Changing society's impression of teaching must be more than sampling the buffet at a Vegas attraction. We can do better.

THE "CHALLENGE CHATS"

Each chapter is accompanied by "Challenge Chats" that bring some highly charged questions and comments to the table. The readers may consider different ways of approaching the "Challenge Chats." The prompts may be addressed in select chapters, depending on the needs and interests of the school or district. There is no need to discuss each question nor complete each chapter chat. The idea is to provoke a deeper dive into select topics. Book study groups, for instance, are also encouraged to generate their own questions to stimulate further discussion.

The Alberta Teachers' Association outlines how book studies can be a viable source of professional growth. They suggest a book study may "consist of four to eight meetings" lasting "between 60 and 90 minutes." They describe the process as choosing a topic that interests everyone in the group "that is sufficiently open-ended to encourage new learning through reading and discussion." They added, "The book should be thought-provoking and have enough depth to stimulate debate."[5]

Whether readers use the "Challenge Chats" prompts or build out customized questions, it is hopeful this text will stimulate rich thought and discussion about the teaching profession and teacher fulfillment. Moreover, this book aims to stretch preconceived notions about what it is educators can do beyond what seems possible.

It may be tempting for some educators to tolerate the current teaching and learning conditions in schools. Some may believe the notion that schools are good enough; all that is needed is a few touch ups. This book addresses why systematic changes are needed and offers ideas for moving forward. Just as Walt Disney needed to be passionate and persistent in his pursuit, so, too, would all stakeholders in education need to be firmly committed to making significant changes necessary to make teaching a highly desirable and sought-after career.

Too frequently, stakeholders accept the gated assumption that they should focus on what they can control. However, the time has come for administrators, teachers, academics, parents, and students to examine the big picture and ideas that may color outside the lines. All schools need not be painted red.

To modify prevailing perceptions of the teaching profession, each challenge can be addressed through a critical and creative lens, one that considers outlier ideas and new job descriptions that have the potency to make teaching one of the most popular careers in the world.

Teachers Shortages and the Challenge of Retention is both a futuristic look at what schooling could be and a reflection on the limitations of current schooling practices. Time is running out, but it is possible to make significant changes, the kind that could make the teaching profession not only a high-demand occupation but work that is perceived by society as meaningful, magical, and memory making.

NOTES

1. Fischer, R. (2004). *The creation of Disneyland*. American Beat. http://www.plosin.com /beatbegins/projects/fischer.html

2. Kamenetz, A. (2022, February 2). *More than half of teachers are looking for the exits, a poll says*. Mind/Shift. https://www.kqed.org/mindshift/59018/more-than-half-of-teachers-are-looking-for-the-exits-a-poll-says

3. Kamenetz, *More than half of teachers*.

4. Sahlberg, P. (2022, June 7). *New Education Minister Jason Clare can fix the teacher shortage crisis—but not with Labor's election plan*. The Conversation. https://theconversation.com/new-education-minister-jason-clare-can-fix-the-teacher-shortage-crisis-but-not-with-labors-election-plan-184321

5. Alberta Teacher's Association. (2023). *PD activities for professional growth.* https://www.teachers.ab.ca/For%20Members/ProfessionalGrowth/Section%203/Pages/Professional%20Development%20Activities%20for%20Teachers.aspx

Chapter 1

Pay Day

> *I'm not an athletic director anymore. I work for a contracting company for the Air Force now! Much, much better pay than working in schools, which sucks because I'd love to still be in schools, but the pay is terrible.*[1]
>
> —Josh Cooper

Josh's mom owned a preschool; he polished floors, moved furniture, and stocked bookshelves to help ready the school for opening. Not only did Josh learn firsthand about the operation of a school, he realized that he wanted to work in education. Josh's education included a master of arts in history degree complete with a varsity lacrosse career. He continues to serve as a member of the U.S. National Guard.

Josh interviewed for a part-time teaching assistant and custodian job at a charter school in Virginia. It was his story about caring for kids and knowing the inner workings of an early childhood center that landed him the position. His work with children was heartfelt; he demonstrated an exceptional level of professionalism, supporting the school in its inaugural year at every turn. Images of Josh wearing a Mario Brothers costume for Halloween was just a glimpse of his commitment to building a positive school culture.

Later Josh aspired to an athletic director position in Virginia. As Josh noted earlier, he is no longer an educator. A husband and father with two children, he needed a respectable salary, and education could not provide him with one. How many other teachers like Josh have left the profession? How many others like Josh would not even consider becoming a teacher because the pay does not equate with the work?

According to the National Education Association in the United States, the average teaching salary was $41,163 in 2019, "with $23,000 difference between the highest and lowest annual starting salary."[2] According to the National Association of Colleges and Employers, the average salary of a university graduate in 2019 was close to $54,000[3]—this figure, lowered by the average teacher salary.

In Canada in 2021, starting salaries varied for each province, but the overall averages ranged between $52,669 and $88,960.[4] Converting to US dollars, these values would be comparable to approximately $39,000 and $65,000. Data compiled from the Organisation for Economic Co-operation and Development (OECD) in 2018 reveals that US elementary teachers with 15 years of experience make, on average, $62,102 annually.[5] Comparatively, Canadian teachers make more ($71,664); Australian teachers average $65,658; and surging to the ranks of supporting the highest-paid teachers is Luxembourg, sporting average salaries after 15 years of $101,360.[6]

Referring to David Cooper's analysis from the Economic Policy Institute (EPI), Kriedler (2022) raised the following concern with regard to trends in teacher pay in California: "When you adjust for inflation, there has been no change in teacher compensation over the past 20 years."[7] To include and cultivate more talent in the teaching profession, schools need to not only simply match the provisions of what other careers provide, schools must consider budgeting for more pay and benefits to generate a much-needed societal shift in perception.

It's not enough anymore to open a box of chocolates on Teacher Appreciation Day. With teacher shortages, it's time for serious budget changes to the bottom line of the teacher's paycheck. Certified teachers who have over five years of higher education should be afforded close to six-figure salaries if they clearly meet the expectations of their job. Teachers who take on additional responsibilities should also be rewarded with ample compensation—much more than a $5,000 stipend for taking on a leadership role such as a high school department head position.

In terms of benefits, Patrick and Carver-Thomas (2022) suggested that federal governments could provide additional incentives:

> While teacher pay levels are a district and state policy decision, there are steps the federal government can take to improve the economic livelihood of teachers. These include creating tax credits for teachers and updating and enhancing existing grant and loan programs to reduce debt for teachers (and other public servants).[8]

To make service industries more appealing, human resources (HR) packages can provide many more attractive features, such as fitness memberships, spa passes, vacation and travel discounts, cell phones, laptops, and funding for future course work and professional learning.

The naysayers who view teachers as greedy may embellish the benefits of teacher time off. The echoes ring loud and clear. What other profession has summers off as well as breaks of three or more weeks a year? Reeves (2018) counters such assumptive talk with the following: "The arguments against a living wage for teachers—they get summers off, they have a six-hour day, and so on—are tired, damaging, and based on false information."[9]

Teachers and those who live with teachers know very well that such time off tends to be used for preparation, as there is not nearly enough provided in each day for coordinating and planning what happens in classrooms. It is probably more accurate to envision teachers with little or no time off, as preparation is a critical component of the job.

Generous benefits packages can attract teaching talent. When increased benefits and mentorship support can be linked to longevity, this can also function as an incentive for teachers. Jason Ablin tweeted, "We need a national center for teachers in their first five years of education. Fully funded. Run by master educators with the goal of . . . guaranteed salaries and benefits if you stay in the classroom for 10+ years."[10]

Concerned about the growing shortage of teachers in Michigan, "the House . . . passed a bill that would provide student teachers a stipend of $90 per day. Experienced teachers who serve as their mentors would receive $1,000."[11] While student teachers may not be certified, they are providing a service on the tutelage of qualified teachers. Much like teaching assistants are paid to support teachers, preservice teachers should also be compensated for their time.

Given teacher certification can take upward of two years after an undergraduate degree, it makes sense to consider paying student teachers for their practicums. It is possible for significant change to happen in education when jurisdictions such as Michigan respond to the current threat of teacher shortages. As Traci Mauriello (2022) noted: "Policymakers are under pressure to make it more affordable for college students to earn education degrees and pay living expenses during student teaching, which can last from a semester to a full year."[12] Faculties of education and school boards really need to consider budgeting to help future teachers in these apprenticeship roles.

Teachers need to be paid professional salaries with ample benefit packages if they are to compete for talent with other professional fields. The law of supply and demand will prevail. School systems can either get ahead of the trend or face the teaching shortage head on. Something significant must be done to make it affordable for teachers to remain. There should be no need for teachers to tutor or wait tables just to make ends meet.

To pay teachers more would require school systems to seriously examine where existing funds can be repurposed and identify where duplicated efforts and other excessive spending is common. According to Patrick and Carver-Thomas (2022),

U.S. teachers generally earn only about 80% of what other college-educated workers earn on a weekly basis. Indeed, among teachers under 40 who left the profession during the pandemic, the top reason identified for their departure was that the pay was insufficient to merit the risk or stress of the job.[13]

The rules for establishing salaries can vary from school to school, but it is time to address the extreme variances in paychecks and benefits. Pay day must reflect the values of the community and respect for the people who teach society's future generation.

CHALLENGE CHAT

- What do you think the ideal teaching wage should be?
- What can school leaders do to support and appreciate teachers?
- What kinds of compensation should be afforded to teachers who take on teacher-leader roles?

NOTES

1. Josh Cooper. (2022, April 15). *I'm not an athletic director anymore. I work for a contracting company for the Air Force now! Much much better pay than working in schools, which sucks because I'd love to still be in schools, but the pay is terrible.* [Direct Message]. Facebook Messenger.

2. Patrick, S. K., & Carver-Thomas, D. (2022, April 14). Teacher salaries: A key factor in recruitment and retention. *Learning Policy Institute.* https://learningpolicyinstitute.org/blog/teacher-salaries-key-factor-recruitment-and-retention

3. National Association of Colleges and Employers. (2020, September 4). *Average salary for class of 2019 up almost 6 percent over class of 2018's.* https://www.naceweb.org/job-market/compensation/average-salary-for-class-of-2019-up-almost-6-percent-over-class-of-2018s/

4. Statistics Canada. (2020). *Table C.3.1. Annual statutory teachers' salaries in public institutions, by level of education taught and teaching experience, Canadian dollars, Canada, provinces and territories, 2018/2019.* https://www150.statcan.gc.ca/n1/pub/81-604-x/2020001/tbl/tblc3.1-eng.htm.

5. OECD. (2018). *Teachers' salaries (indicator).* https://data.oecd.org/eduresource/teachers-salaries.htm

6. OECD, *Teachers' salaries (indicator).*

7. Kreidler, M. (2022, June 2). *California public schools are losing underpaid teachers at a steep rate.* Capital and Main. https://capitalandmain.com/california-public-schools-are-losing-underpaid-teachers-at-a-steep-rate

8. Patrick & Carver-Thomas, Teacher salaries.

9. Reeves, D. B. (2018, May 1). Seven keys to restoring the teacher pipeline. *ASCD*. https://www.ascd.org/el/articles/seven-keys-to-restoring-the-teacher-pipeline

10. Ablin, J. [@JasonAblin]. (2022, May 7). *We need a national center for teachers in their first five years of education. Fully funded. Run by master educators.* [Tweet]. Twitter. https://twitter.com/search?q=We%20need%20a%20national%20center%20for%20teachers%20in%20their%20first%20five%20years%20of%20education.%20Fully%20funded.%20Run%20by%20master%20educators&src=typed_query&f=top

11. Mauriello, T. (2022, June 15). *Michigan House passes bill to pay student teachers for classroom work*. Bridge Michigan. https://www.bridgemi.com/talent-education/michigan-house-passes-bill-pay-student-teachers-classroom-work

12. Mauriello, *Michigan House passes bill.*

13. Patrick & Carver-Thomas, Teacher Salaries.

Chapter 2

Significantly Reducing Class Size

I've said it before and I'll say it again: it blows my mind how manageable a class is when I have 4 to 5 less students in it.[1]

—@saneELAteacher

Whether teachers have 30 students, 25, or even 20 in their classes, most instinctively know that if they had at least four or five fewer students, they could be more effective with reduced classroom sizes. Imagine what learning and engagement would happen if teachers had to manage 10 to 14 students? Debates can continue about the ideal class size, but if school leaders recall their days in the classroom, they should agree that fewer students is better.

While some administrative research may negate the need to reduce class size, there is a sound curriculum argument for fewer students. Based on constructivist models for teaching and learning, students can move from novice levels of understanding to more expert levels when they have ample opportunities to interact with their teachers. Fewer students in a class gives students more time with the teacher to experience such apprenticeship learning.

Students in apprentice roles need to speak with experts in order to appropriate language and use it to emulate experts. When students have to wait their turn, there is a reduced opportunity for each student in a class to master the subject matter.

Vygotsky's classic view of learning in his "zone of proximal development" (ZPD)[2] theory emphasizes the importance of students having time to interact with experts in order to appropriate the actions and language of experts. Lave and Wenger's work stressed that learning required "legitimate peripheral participation" (LPP)[3] to move students from novice to apprentice to expert learners.

Internships provide ideal learning conditions, as the expert and learner have ample time to interact, which is vastly different from a classroom context where students have to share the "air time" with their classmates.

Progressive school systems will make room for internship experiences, but they must also reduce class sizes if they are serious about improving student and teacher engagement and learning.

Textbooks, void of talk, can be far too removed to promote deep learning and interaction. While such resources can provide reference points and contexts for discussions, they are not as powerful as a teacher working and speaking with a student directly and in ways that enable learners to elaborate on their understandings—beyond the shallow, single-word response that teachers of classes with 20 or more students must endure.

Reducing class sizes and increasing teacher-to-student interactions should minimize the demand for elaborate restorative behavioral modification programs. Often, schools approach discipline problems by resting the blame on students or their home life. Focusing on behavioral symptoms or assuming the causes of apathy or disengagement arise from forces outside of school can appear to be an active response, but it can narrow the field of options for improving teaching and learning conditions.

While it is important to recognize the negative impact of cycles of violence or conditions of poverty, schools must look to what they can control as well. How many school leaders actually examine the possibility that some disruptive behavior might be influenced by systematic policies and practices within the school itself?

While supports are needed to help all students, schools need to consider systematic changes to reduce a growing critical mass of students, who are making it difficult for classrooms to be engaging and industrious. It's too simple to blame disruptive behavior on the pandemic, on parents who may not have the same disciplinary style as the teacher during the lockdown at home, or on a lack of resources. How schools design the context for learning can make a difference, especially when there is significant time afforded to develop quality teacher and student relationships.

Reducing the number of students in classes should also limit the exploding demand for tutoring programs. Students and parents know that this smaller teaching and learning unit is required to enhance and supplement what the typical classroom size cannot. The growth of the tutoring industry is a testimony to the need for deeper interaction opportunities, which a traditional classroom cannot provide. Schools need a new normal and ways to use time differently in a new age of schooling.

Many elementary and, in some cases, high school subject teachers can take part in looping practices, whereby teachers have students for two or three years in a row. Coordinating schedules so that students can be with teachers for more than a year can benefit both students and teachers. The time gained for teachers in not having to start over to build new relationships every year can reduce the workload but also help students to not have so many new teaching faces and styles to decipher year after year.

Funds from federal recovery programs, special grants, or other "additional" funding sources should be recognized for what they are—a temporary Band-Aid or short-term stimulus solutions. Working conditions that accept large class sizes as business as usual are not addressing a serious deterrent in the profession.

Funding formulas for schools must change if teachers are going to work in more fulfilling environments that are conducive to enhancing teaching and learning. Furthermore, it is important to identify schools with underserved populations to ensure they can receive more financial support. Budgets need to be repurposed, and funds from one area of a school budget must be moved to provide for increased staffing so that teaching talent can do work that is doable and fulfilling. It is possible to restructure schools to reduce the teaching load and capacity to support all students to master learning.

CHALLENGE CHAT

- In what ways does your school reduce class sizes?
- What would be the barriers to reducing class sizes?
- How could staff roles be revised to help reduce class sizes?
- How often does each teacher contribute in a staff meeting with more than 10 people in attendance?

NOTES

1. That ELA teacher [@saneELAteacher]. (2022, April 26). *I've said it before and I'll say it again: it blows my mind how manageable a class is when I*. [Tweet]. Twitter. https://twitter.com/saneELAteacher/status/1518971342229590017

2. Vygotsky, L. S. (1978). *Mind in society: The development of higher psychological processes*. Cambridge, MA: Harvard University Press.

3. Lave, J., & Wenger, E. (1991). *Situated learning: Legitimate peripheral participation*. Cambridge, UK: Cambridge University Press.

Chapter 3

Time to Polish, Prepare, and Reflect

Teachers need planning time to think about, sketch, physically set up (and take down), and reassess daily teaching practices and whole units. Without this time we're left scrambling to photocopy workbooks from 1999. Boring.[1]

—Kyleen Gray

Gray's analysis is spot on. In a letter penned to school administrators, she begins, "Amazing pedagogical practice isn't created overnight. It's curated during bits and pieces of planning time strewn together into engaging lessons, units, and long-term plans that effectively reflect curriculum expectations."[2] Whether written before, after, or, in this case, in the thick of the COVID storm, teachers needed and still need ample planning time to work on their own and with their colleagues to be effective.

According to Sahlberg, "A recent Grattan Institute study reported 86% of all teachers feel they don't have enough time for planning and collaboration at school."[3] When asked to share ideas about ideal conditions for teacher preparation, early childhood educator Lori Fuchs (2022) noted:

> It would be uninterrupted. Too often the prep time is taken over by meetings, covering something, or other administrative tasks. There would be an understanding that prep looks different for different teachers. Teacher A might want the time to grade papers, Teacher B might answer e-mails, Teachers C & D might collaborate on a lesson plan.[4]

What is often presented on a schedule and what actually happens in prep times can often not be in alignment. As education consultant Hope Blecher acknowledged:

This prep period has become non-existent for some educators. Why? Because of the shortage of teachers and substitutes, the existing teachers are assigned classes to cover. Sometimes, that is paid, sometimes it isn't; paying doesn't compensate for the missed prep period when it happens over and over again.[5]

Teachers need time to think and plan individually and with others. Grade meetings are often based on the assumption that students should be working on the same page at the same time in different classes within the same grade. This does not make sense, as Fuchs has added, "Until the schools recognize that in order to differentiate and meet the needs of the students in a given class, not every class will look or sound the same. They will not be on the same page and that is a good thing!"[6] Cap Lee (2022) suggested that schools should organize planning for integrated project work around block times with teachers, educational assistants, and/or special education teachers "to determine the student schedule on a daily basis."[7] He added that "if higher ups want to count the minutes for each, let them try."[8]

The need for substantial preparation time begs the question, How much is enough? What is clear is that, in many cases, the amount of time provided and the way the time is used is not sufficient. Teachers need professional time to breath, grow, and plan for the coming week. Time can be a tool for rejuvenating the teaching profession, but courage is required for school decision makers to risk how it can be redistributed throughout the day, week, month, and school year.

School leaders also need to look beyond the compartmentalized school year, beyond calculating the adding on of minutes in a school day or at the end of the school year. A quality education should not be defined by the quantitative chunking of minute formulas, assuming time to be the gatekeeper of equity. Spreading a realistic workload over five days can be an option that can provide teachers more time to prepare quality lesson or project experiences. Teachers need significant blocks of time to prepare individually and collectively.

Many schools may check off the boxes that their teacher grade teams meet weekly for an hour, but how valuable is such time, when three or more professionals have to share air time in a confined time space? If students could be dismissed early from their formal learning program on at least a monthly basis, teachers could have at least two hours to engage in more stimulating, meaningful, and productive co-planning, far more effective than a token period churned out in a typically weekly school schedule.

With additional time, teachers can not only be more aware of what other teachers are doing and assigning, they can have time to coordinate integrated and interdisciplinary projects or build detailed action plans to support students in need of additional support. Teachers would have more time to examine student work and adapt instruction to meet the individual needs of each student.

Teachers also need professional learning days for viewing progressive practices outside their school and classrooms. At some schools, principals arrange for or support teachers to visit classrooms in other schools, and the teachers sometimes return to see the same teacher or view a variety of teachers to gain a deeper understanding of the range of practices and contexts. Unfortunately, there are too many teachers who do not have such opportunities.

Professional learning can involve examining current research and informed practices as well as conducting action research. When teachers become researchers and examine evidence of learning in their classrooms, they become empowered about their profession. Each school and classroom context is unique, and while textbooks and curriculum guides may provide general ideas, a teacher who makes sense of their classrooms can contribute to the direction rather than follow a shallow plan not specific for any classroom.

Fifth grade teacher Lisa Hudson (2022) offered the advice that schools should coordinate schedules where teachers work directly with students on Monday through Thursday but use Fridays for planning. She clarified that planning days should not be filled with "useless PD or meetings," having added that teacher teams can meet if needed—but not because it is some mandatory requirement. Lisa echoed her desire for more autonomy: "Allow me to decide what to do with my planning time, whether it's grading, planning, gathering resources."[9]

Referring to her teaching experiences in four- and five-day schools, Martina Cahill noted, "Teacher and student burn out was far less of an issue than at five day schools."[10] Few teachers can make such a comparison, but teacher Cahill, who worked in a farming community, can. She explained that some rural schools turned to four-day weeks "to retain teachers," having added, "smaller districts compete with city districts, or small rural towns struggle to get teachers to remain in their districts because they can't compete with raises, benefits."[11]

To counter the argument that students would learn less, Cahill added, "We consistently had the second highest test scores in the district, and second only to . . . the other four-day school in the district."[12] How productive can teachers in typical five-day schools be when the ratio of prep time to teaching time is approximately 12 to 1? A four-day week could change that ratio significantly.

Cahill also recalled how she never took a day off in the three years she worked in the four-day school. She mentioned that it wasn't "because I was crazy, but because I could schedule anything I needed for Friday afternoons."[13] She added, "Fridays are also the day most staff members tend to take their days in five day schools, because it's just easiest. I never had to do that."[14] It seems reasonable to assume that high teacher absenteeism rates reflect unrealistic demands of the job.

According to the author of the book *Rest,* Dr. Alex Soojung-Kim Pang, "Employers should think less about time spent working and more about quality. He has identified about 130 employers, including Kickstarter and the government of Iceland, that have adopted a four-day, reduced-hour week without cutting salaries or sacrificing productivity."[15] He explained that each person has a personalized rhythm that does not conform to a nine-to-five work schedule.

When the idea of a four-day week was posed on *LinkedIn*, many educators tuned in, including primary teacher Dan Robinson, who said, "It would be mind blowingly powerful."[16]

Time and work researcher Dr. Dawna Ballard from the University of Texas claimed that people are more productive when they can work on their own schedules, noting that our current system is how machines work (but not humans), making a point that humans break down.[17] Schools are pushing the boundaries of productivity for students and teachers.

Referring to a cultural shift to a four-day school week, Cahill noted:

> I may have been naive to think that everyone would love the idea of a four-day school, but people are actually pretty against it at first . . . In general, parents and families are about 50/50 when schools decide to try to go to a four-day. Half are for it and half are against it. *But,* after one year of being [in] four-day schools, satisfactions surveys show that 90%–95% of families are satisfied with the switch.[18]

When schools consider making serious changes, there can be considerable upheaval.

Any alternative to the status quo ultimately can be met with resistance, even though educators realize that change is a vital component of improvement. To explore a four-day work week by cramming five days of content into four would be a stress-inducing approach that makes no sense, especially if school systems are serious about addressing teacher and student wellness.

Cahill's frank voice addresses the notion that many teachers in typical five-day schools take a monthly personal day or more to catch up, refresh, or tread water for a time, before getting back into the marathon reality of teaching. How is such absentee data interpreted, and what are school systems doing about it? The timing of teaching and learning is simply not working.

Cahill's lens presents some powerful alternatives to school design with ways of distributing time differently.

Changing school schedules would undoubtedly disrupt the status quo—but not as much as not having quality teachers be present in schools. How do schools use time to reduce teacher burnout? The random allocation of preparation time requires further examination particularly in light of teacher shortages and recent concerns raised by teachers exiting the profession.

Who is conducting these exit interviews, and what are school systems doing about such data? The current use of time in schools does not meet the needs of many teachers and students, and it is time to consider, create, and plan for new schools that blend wellness and learning for all.

Teacher burnout is and has been a serious issue in education. The recent pandemic functioned as a tipping point that pushed many more educators towards officially exiting the profession, but the harsh reality of lagging morale was already too commonplace in schools well before COVID. Too many teachers feel they do not have time to polish, prepare, and reflect on their teaching.

The idea of significantly reducing instructional time could be a deal breaker; the sooner school systems consider piloting material changes in scheduling, the sooner teachers can have a fighting chance at fulfillment, and the sooner more potential teachers might gravitate toward the field. Working conditions that do not permit for adequate preparation, refinement of one's craft, and opportunities to reflect on practice are not serving teachers nor students.

When a typical teacher has upward of thirty classes each week, each should require an equitable amount of time for preparation. The numbers, however, do not add up. There isn't enough time in most schedules for both instruction and preparation. Professionals in many other fields can spend weeks preparing for one presentation. And many other professionals can have teams of people preparing viewgraphs and handouts for them.

Imagine what the quality of teaching would be like if teachers were treated as professionals and given the time they need to prepare quality work? The sharp contrast between teacher expectations and what other professionals do is worthy of further discussions and deeper thought.

Tyler Rablin shared, "Every single school should be working to figure out how to double plan time for teachers."[19] Teachers need time to prepare and polish their craft. One planning period per day for 45 minutes plus three professional learning days a year is not enough. To be exceptional, teachers wind up using their personal time in the evening hours, breaks, and summer to properly plan for their classes. Teacher shortages are now more than the tip of a burnout iceberg.

What if teachers had more time to balance and meet expectations? Would they have more energy to be abreast of current research, take part in recess duty, manage the library, supervise a stamp club, or coach a sports team? Would they be committed to further professional growth, teacher leadership roles, and make meaningful connections with parents? What if teachers were given one day a week for preparation in addition to their daily planning period, with wellness breaks throughout the day plus an hour lunch?

The lived experiences of four-day work weeks do not seem to be the target of educational research or many expert recommendations, which may perhaps be too timid and shy away from such disruptive change. Nevertheless, there are few examples of the four-day week in education that have survived the test of time. In some rural districts in the United States, there have been cases where schools implemented fewer days to accommodate the need for farm workers, reduce schooling costs, and attract teachers willing to work fewer hours.

There is never enough time for students to memorize the encyclopedia of all there is to know. For over half a century, curriculum experts have sounded the alarm that such a goal is ridiculous, no matter how much slick software can spit out practice-test curriculum aimed at ranking and separating the *Jeopardy* champions of the day. The four-day work week is an opportunity for schools to determine what is essential and concurrently build in time for teachers to design curriculum that enables learning to stick.

For some the fifth day could be used for quality replenishing and restocking of a teacher's energy shelves. They might coordinate action research or curriculum design, or spend time to meet with other teachers inside or outside the school. It could be time afforded to change up the classroom bulletin boards to showcase evidence of student learning and recognize the depth and breadth of student creativity. It could be time to read about current research or write meaningful messages to families.

Whether schools implement four-day weeks, early dismissals, and/or continue with professional learning days, it is important to look for ways to ensure that students are safe and supervised, especially when many families have fixed 40-hour work weeks. Changes to school time would impact the need for alternative supports to account for the time differential between typical and revised dismissal times. The safety and care of children must be of paramount concern.

Schools could work with community agencies to provide special programming for students, as working families may not be able to find additional or affordable childcare. Budgeting to support such programming would need to add significant new line items, as there would be real costs associated with internal professional planning and ongoing school improvement activities.

A former alumnus of Crossroads Christian High School in California, Brandon Oddo shared the following recollection about his experience in textbox 3.1.

Sustaining progressive education initiatives is not easy. Oddo acknowledged that the school now faces several struggles, including

TEXTBOX 3.1: ACCOUNT OF EXPERIENCE AT CROSSROADS CHRISTIAN HIGH SCHOOL

I was blessed to be part of a very special high school and to be the pioneering class. It was a small (~100 students) private school, and I do think that setting played a large role in what the school was able to accomplish.

It was a 21st century, collaborative curriculum, so we had MacBooks instead of textbooks and did a lot of team projects. We had a block schedule with two major classes a day: one pair of classes on Monday and Thursday, the other pair on Tuesday and Friday. The classes were integrated subjects (i.e., an English plus history class and a science plus math class). Each class utilized a mostly flipped-classroom approach, so we would have videos or readings from the day before and then reinforcement of material, question time, and application in the class. We also had four units a semester and would be part of one new team per unit.

That team would have four projects to do—one for each class—so we were doing 16 projects a semester ranging from PowerPoint presentations to iMovies to group essays to construction projects, and so on. Wednesdays, then, were a time for us to do any flipped-classroom work or to meet with our teams and work on projects. Each team also kept track of an "Action Plan" where we'd document daily tasks, what was accomplished, and group feedback . . . We were also graded individually on the team projects so that the whole team wouldn't have their grades hurt if one member was consistently not fulfilling their tasks.

At the end of each day, we had a fine arts block. Everyone was required to be in one of the fine arts teams: the cast, tech, marketing, hair/makeup/costume, house, and on. The teams were meant to provide a sort of training wheels version of a job. Students had to apply into the team, would obtain promotions to managerial positions, had inter-department meetings . . . By our senior year, we had a surprising amount of autonomy and spent large chunks of the day doing personal projects and independent studies.[20]

- translating their approach to a larger scale;
- keeping teachers happy with salaries and benefits comparable to public schools;
- finding staff that fully buy into the mission and can execute it well; and,

- trying to include students that can't afford the full tuition.[21]

Even though there was ample preparation time in such innovative institutions, there are many other pieces of the job-satisfaction puzzle that need to fall into place for students and teachers to thrive.

According to the Brookings Institute estimate, "About 660 schools in 24 states were using four-day weeks before the pandemic caused school closures in 2020." At One City Schools in Wisconsin, students from preschool to fourth grade go to school five days a week, but teachers only work a four-day week. "It's a model that takes into account . . . the impact of a shorter week on student learning and gaps in childcare that might otherwise come up."[22]

Iceland piloted the four-day work week with 2,500 public service employees between 2015 and 2019. According to Anna Cooban (2022), "Those trials found no corresponding drop in productivity—and a dramatic increase in employee well-being."[23]

More recently, in the United Kingdom, thousands of employees are testing out the four-day work schedule with no cut to their pay. Cooban noted, "The six-month pilot commits 3,300 workers across 70 companies to work 80% of their usual week in exchange for promising to maintain 100% of their productivity."[24] Cooban added that the extra day "made space for many workers to take up new hobbies, fulfill longstanding ambitions, or simply invest more time in their relationships. Workers on the trial have taken up cooking classes, piano lessons, volunteering, fishing and rollerskating."[25]

As more and more conditions for ideal teaching and learning emerge, the question is not so much which variable matters the most but, rather, how each component enriches the whole of the profession. It could be argued that even if only one condition is not addressed, it will minimize the overall return of cultivating a deeply fulfilled teaching culture.

Time is precious in society, but most people do not recognize the unrealistic expectations of time demands on teachers. Computers were supposed to make things easier, but it could be argued that without a thoughtful coordination of technology with expectations, it can contribute to the madness.

Deliberately disrupting the way time is distributed in schools could change the culture of everyone in them. Administrators can count minutes to ensure equity while the ship continues on a course toward a pending iceberg, or they can make serious changes happen—the potent kind that gives teachers reasons to stay and makes the profession more attractive for newcomers.

CHALLENGE CHAT

- Do you think teachers could plan better with fewer classes to teach in a week?
- Given Mondays tend to house the most holidays, what if the school year was designed with the other Mondays as *professional growth days*, with students having special elective programming and micro-credential learning options?
- Would teachers participate more in action or independent research if there was a dedicated time each week for such professional growth activity?
- Draw and label an image of how you might carve up time for a teacher in a day, week, month, and school year.
- Are you aware if your school's strategic plan is aiming to reduce instructional hours and increase professional learning hours?
- What would you like to see added or taken away from your school or school district's strategic plan?

NOTES

1. Gray, K. (2019, October 22). Dear school administrators, please stop taking away teacher planning periods. *We Are Teachers*. https://www.weareteachers.com/i-need-my-planning-periods/

2. Gray, *Dear school administrators*.

3. Sahlberg, P. (2022, June 7). New education minister Jason Clare can fix the teacher shortage crisis but not with labors election plan. *The Conversation*. https://theconversation.com/new-education-minister-jason-clare-can-fix-the-teacher-shortage-crisis-but-not-with-labors-election-plan-184321

4. Fuchs, L. (2022, May 13). *It would be uninterrupted. Too often the prep time is taken over by meetings, covering something, or other administrative tasks.* [Post]. LinkedIn. https://www.linkedin.com/in/lori-fuchs-m-ed-6644a3179/recent-activity/

5. (H. Blecher, email personal communication, July 17, 2022).

6. Fuchs, *It would be uninterrupted*.

7. Lee, C. (2022, May 13). *First there would be block time with 2 teachers, ed assistant and/or sp ed to determine the student schedule on*. [Post]. LinkedIn. https://www.linkedin.com/in/cap-lee-914831/recent-activity/

8. Lee, *First there would be block*.

9. Hudson, L. [@LisaMim89838138]. (2022, May 13). *Teach Monday-Thursday, plan on Friday. Don't full planning day with useless PD or meetings. Teams meet if needed, not*. [Post]. LinkedIn. https://www.linkedin.com/in/lmims/recent-activity/

10. Cahill, M. (2022, May 13). The four-day school week: Everything you wanted to know. *The Hungry Teacher Blog*. https://thehungryteacherblog.com/2018/03/the-four-day-school-week.html

11. Cahill, The four-day school week.
12. Cahill, The four-day school week.
13. Cahill, The four-day school week.
14. Cahill, The four-day school week.
15. Soojung-Kim Pang, A. (2018). *Rest: Why you get more done when you work less.* New York: Basic Books.
16. Robinson, D. (2022, February 20). *It would be mind blowingly powerful.* [personal communication]. LinkedIn. https://www.linkedin.com/in/daniel-robinson-teacher/recent-activity/
17. Laber-Warren, E. (2022, March 17). The 9-to-5 schedule should be the next pillar of work to fall. *The New York Times.* https://www.nytimes.com/2022/03/17/opinion/work-flexibility-hours.html
18. Cahill, The four-day school week.
19. Rablin, T. [@Mr_Rablin]. (2022, May 30). *Every single school should be working to figure out how to double plan time for teachers. The US requires more.* [Tweet]. Twitter. https://twitter.com/Mr_Rablin/status/1531386199314616321
20. (B. Oddo, email personal communication, May 16, 2022).
21. Oddo, email personal communication.
22. Tamez-Robledo, N. (2022, June 22). Can four-day school weeks keep teachers from leaving? *EdSurge.* https://www.edsurge.com/news/2022-06-22-can-four-day-school-weeks-keep-teachers-from-leaving
23. Cooban, A. (2022, August 1). How the world's biggest four-day workweek trial run changed people's lives. CNN Business. https://www.cnn.com/2022/08/01/business/4-day-work-week-uk-trial/index.html
24. Cooban, *How the world's biggest four-day workweek.*
25. Cooban, *How the world's biggest four-day workweek.*

Chapter 4

Time to Teach and Learn

> *Although working in a good state school, the reality of my role as a teacher equated to endless bureaucracy and tick-box testing. Most of the opportunities for holistic development were stripped bare and ground down to a series of "objectives to be covered."*[1]
>
> —Kimberley Cooper

As a new teacher, Kimberley was full of ideas and eager to "make a difference"; her enthusiasm was initially paused by bureaucracy. Fortunately, Kimberley's story is not a loss, as she was able to find work in a more progressive school that valued 21st-century and holistic learning. Her transformational work as an educational writer and influencer contributes a valuable voice of hope for a better education.

Like Kimberley, teachers who recognize the value of deep learning are well aware of the need for time to introduce a lesson with ample chances for all students to apply their learning and have intensive opportunities to be enriched by each classroom experience. This is impossible to do in 40- to 45-minute time slots, but such limited time spans often contribute to increased numbers of bored students, who do not have time to engage and interact with the subject matter.

The schedule should not take precedence over learning; anything less than 60 minutes for most classes is minimizing the opportunity for all students to learn. Even with small class sizes, it can be impossible to check for understanding when the class length does not permit teachers to grapple with ideas with each student. Some teachers may be comfortable with smaller, teacher-directed units of time, but overall satisfaction can be much more when students have the time they need to demonstrate what they know.

According to author and speaker Suzanne DeMallie, teachers need more time within their workday to do the things they need to do in order to be a better teacher. So much of what a teacher needs to do in order to effectively teach, has to currently be done on their own time—after school, before school, nights, and weekends—quickly leading to teacher burnout.[2]

Just as teachers need time to grapple with ideas, apply their understandings, and construct new ways of supporting student (and their own) learning, students also need ample time to master concepts and skills. Time is needed for teachers to integrate informed teaching and learning approaches such as *habits of mind*[3] and *multi-intelligences*,[4] experiences that help all students come to solid understandings.

Many teachers who have time to reflect on their practice realize the potency of teaching as a way of learning. The more teachers talk, the more they construct meaning; conversely, the more time they take up in class doing the talking, the less students have rich opportunities to appropriate expert language. The teacher-directed classroom tends to have the teacher formulating questions with students contributing single-word or simple-phrase responses, leading to limited opportunities for elaboration that are missed with such well-intended efforts at inclusion.

Peer teaching, where older students teach younger students, is a powerful learning experience that puts "teaching" (with adult guidance) as a learning approach in the hands of students. Schools that promote learning buddies for reading, writing, math, or other subject areas recognize the inherent value of making time for such potent practices. It can be so rewarding for many teachers to have time systematically built into their week to observe their students interact with other students, yet such opportunities for fulfillment tend to be few and far between.

Time for teaching should include time for quality student feedback, formatively and formally. While each student may be a novice when learning new concepts, they are unique in how much time they need and what kinds of conditions they require to move to an expert level of understanding. When the same time frames for learning are mandated for all students, there is a misguided assumption that all students require the same time and lesson to achieve mastery.

Room in the form of time must be provided for students to experience learning in multiple ways. Teachers cannot provide such customized supports when the curriculum is stuffed past capacity. Teachers cannot prepare every meal on the menu for every student, nor can each student eat every item on the menu at the same time. Teachers should be trusted as curriculum designers to determine what is essential and, in doing so, have the autonomy to prepare meaningful and fulfilling teaching and learning experiences.

Even when teaching time is stripped of applied or creative ways of engaging students in learning, there is not enough time to cover the various curricula. It can be so jammed packed, it smothers the potential for deep thinking. How often do teachers echo that there is not enough time in the day? Within the current structures, they are quite correct; there is not enough time for informed practice.

What kind of 40-hour work week could a future school look like? Table 4.1 illustrates a sample schedule for a grade three English language arts (ELA) and social studies teacher that provides time for preparation and ongoing professional learning. Ample time for growth can happen when the 40-hour work week is broken down with fewer instructional hours than what is typically commonplace in schools. The week could be broken down as follows in this classroom:

- 10 hours of instructional classes
- 3.75 to 5 hours per week for wellness breaks
- 2.5 hours for homeroom
- 2.5 hours of lunch
- 2 hours of mentor meetings
- 2 to 3 hours of supervision
- 13 to 16 hours of prep for professional growth (PG)

There is no magic formula for the ideal schedule, but the lack of time for preparing and growing is a serious concern. The day, structure, and organization of school needs to change if teachers are going to be given realistic conditions for success. Schools need to use time differently if they expect higher levels of student and teacher engagement.

CHALLENGE CHAT

- According to JFK, "We must use time as a tool, not as a crutch." How is time a crutch in schools, and what can be done about it?
- How do teachers find more time to apply practices that support building creative and critical thinking classroom experiences?
- On a weekly basis, how often are students in classrooms engaged in project-based learning (regularly, sometimes, not at all)? Discuss.
- How often do students take part in formalized peer-teaching or buddy-learning scenarios (weekly, a few times a year, random, not at all)? Discuss.

Table 4.1: Sample Grade Three ELA and Social Studies Teacher

	Monday	Tuesday	Wednesday	Thursday	Friday
8:00 a.m.			Gr. 3 Homeroom		
8:30 a.m.	Prep/PG	Prep/PG	Prep/PG	ELA	Prep/PG
9:30 a.m.	Prep/PG	Prep/PG	Prep/PG	Prep/PG	Prep/PG
10:15 a.m.	Recess Supervision	Recess Supervision	Recess Supervision	Recess Supervision	Recess Supervision
10:30 a.m.	Wellness Break	Wellness Break	Wellness Break	Wellness Break	Wellness Break
11:30 a.m.			Lunch		
12:15 p.m.	ELA	ELA	ELA	Gr. 3 Team Planning with ELA Mentor	ELA
1:00 p.m.	ELA	ELA	ELA	Gr. 3 Team Teaching with ELA Mentor	ELA
1:45 p.m.	Recess Supervision	Recess Supervision	Recess Supervision	Recess Supervision	Recess Supervision
2:00 p.m.	Social Studies	ELA	Social Studies	ELA	Social Studies
3:00 p.m.	Dismissal Supervision	Dismissal Supervision	Dismissal Supervision	Dismissal Supervision	Dismissal Supervision

- On a weekly basis, how much individual contact could each student receive, and for how long would sustained interaction be between teacher and student with each contact?
- Does your school change the schedule to improve teaching and learning conditions for students and teachers?
- What do you think happens to teachers who do not have time to prepare for quality teaching and learning experiences?
- What are schools doing to listen and respond to the voices of committed educators?

NOTES

1. Cooper, K. (2002, February). Do our children deserve better? *Holistic Learning*. https://holisticlearning.co.uk/do-our-children-deserve-better/

2. DeMallie, S. (2022, February). *More time within their workday to do the things they need to do in order to be a better teacher*. [Post]. LinkedIn. https://www.linkedin.com/in/suzanne-demallie/recent-activity/

3. Habits of Mind. (2022). *What are the habits of mind?* The Institute for Habits of Mind. https://www.habitsofmindinstitute.org/what-are-habits-of-mind/

4. Harvard Graduate School of Education. (2022). *Multiple intelligences*. Project Zero. http://www.pz.harvard.edu/projects/multiple-intelligences

Chapter 5

Time for Robust Professional Learning

I am far from the defender of all things PD. I have sat in on many hours of "development" that I consider to be virtually useless. With that being said, I have to . . . point out that some of the pushback against PD is, in fact, teachers just not wanting to develop or change.[1]

—Andrew Pillow

Mr. Pillow's (2021) voice reveals the reality of pushback against professional development as linked to a pattern of resisting change or being nonresponsive to it. He added,

I have been teaching for over a decade, and more times than I can count, I have witnessed teachers sleepwalk and complain about PD they were forced to attend, only to struggle in the area covered during the school year.[2]

It's time for professional development (PD) to plan for a facelift. As Fullan noted, "Professional development as a term and as a strategy has run its course," adding that "we must abandon professional development and make professional learning an everyday experience for all educators."[3]

In order to change mindsets about the value of professional learning, school leaders need to unpack and compare effective and less effective professional growth activity practices. How to design a continuous learning context for teachers that moves the sleepwalkers to skippers should be part of a genuine overall educational pursuit for excellence.

Robust professional learning needs to be meaningful, relevant, and responsive while grounded in evidence-based practice. Too much and too many disconnected initiatives can do more harm than good.

Moreover, teachers need time to implement and adapt new approaches prompted by professional learning, based on their own classroom needs. Teachers need dedicated time for professional growth activities. Rather than view PD as a noun, it makes more sense to address PD as a verb, noting that ongoing growth means teachers are professionally developing, adapting, responding, and improving throughout their career.

Just as Dewey (1907) claimed that students are not empty vessels to fill with knowledge,[4] school leaders need to approach teachers as valuable contributors who can do much more than teach a paint-by-numbers curriculum. When PD is pushed at teachers without their input and not as a genuine opportunity to respond and reshape ideas to meet their classroom needs, it can be perceived as just another initiative. Teachers, who have opportunities to coconstruct units and lessons, will be empowered and take more ownership over the recommended changes.

Coupled with a clear direction that supports individual and collective school goals, teachers can be inspired to continue developing through daily, weekly, monthly, term, annual, and multiyear professional activity. Additionally, it is common practice for many teachers to take part in professional development activities at the end of the school year and for at least a week prior to the first day of school.

Pre-kindergarten and science teacher Ashley (Almonte) Lopez mentioned that she experienced "fantastic opportunities for professional development,"[5] appreciating access to readings from experts such as Dr. David Booth. She was particularly grateful for the opportunity to attend "Harvard Project Zero" (PZ) with eleven other colleagues. She noted the following:

> This experience was an emotional one that allowed us to build on previous experiences and expand on our capabilities as educators. We were excited to share what we learned during our weeklong professional development before the school year began and arranged for small teacher study groups to learn about and implement the various skills we took from PZ.[6]

Referring to how the PZ experience lived back in her school, Ashley noted,

> Throughout that school year, teachers excitedly implemented new PZ strategies, including Artful Thinking, Brain Dance, and Reggio Emilia routines. The idea of "Taming the Wild and Wilding the Tame" took our school by storm as we made learning a more hands-on and interactive experience for everyone involved.[7]

Quality experiences that support teaching professionals in their ongoing quest for improvement should happen before school, during school, after school, and on a daily reflective basis. A carefully designed plan for professional growth requires school leaders to make time for PD activities in- and outside the school setting.

SELF-REVIEW ON A DAILY BASIS

Every day a teacher needs time to reflect and revise future plans for teaching. While many expert teachers can adapt while the class is in play, all teachers require time to design and redesign the landscape of teaching and learning on a daily basis. A rigid lesson plan should not be a fixed set of activities, defined by some arbitrary time limits. It should not be assumed that teachers can reflect on their instructional choices during wellness or lunch breaks. There needs to be dedicated time for such ongoing growth that emerges from a daily self-examination of professional practice.

PROFESSIONAL LEARNING DAYS—
BEFORE SCHOOL BEGINS

The preparation for every school opening involves time for staff to organize their classroom and make teaching materials on their own and with their colleagues. Outside the classroom preparation, there are schoolwide practices and policies that the staff need to know and understand. There are usually updates to safety protocols, the school calendar, and often new staff members to welcome into the community. The professional learning before school starts should weave together individual, collective, and school operational needs with significant opportunities to build genuine social relationships.

Staff members should not feel isolated from the adults in the school, so such an experience should be just as much about team building as inspiring teaching and learning activities. At one school, new teachers were paired up with seasoned teachers, who took them first on a blindfolded tour of the school. They repeated the tour without blindfolds, giving new teachers ample time to talk with and get to know at least one staff member. Some schools build in retreats to spas or block off teambuilding days for ziplining and ropes circuits.

Experts are often invited as guest speakers to support professional learning. At one school the local police chief and a parent who worked at the CIA took the school through a simulation-lockdown procedure and shared a review, as well as a Q&A of the school's safety and crisis management protocols. Some schools coordinate some PD activities with other schools or invite parents to join PD sessions. Alfie Kohn's presentations on homework are particularly informative.

At a PK to grade eight performing arts school in Washington, DC, the staff was organized in groups using the names from the Broadway show themes of one year, followed by tickets and popcorn the next year, fitting with an "at the movies" theme. One PD program was designed as a "playbill," with tickets created for various events throughout the week. Raffle tickets for gift cards encouraged staff to bring and add to their portfolios the takeaways from academic book clubs, vertical subject matter essential skills meetings, and ideas for creating their own project-based resources.

To ensure the school handbook was understood, staff at one school were asked to submit questions for a quiz show about the staff handbook. Staff should have opportunities to interact with PD messages. When beginning strategic planning work at one school, the staff were organized in small groups to draw and label qualities of an ideal school in preparation, which were shared and posted. The staff were asked to view each image and add a colored sticky dot to indicate which ideas they liked the most. When students arrived, they had a chance to view these images as well.

WEEKLY COMMUNICATION

Apart from regular, face-to-face PD activities, every communication can function as a source for professional growth. Weekly Friday fliers, weekend updates, or, in the case at one school, I penned *Barb's Bundles* to collate not only information but also support shout-outs as ongoing recognition for staff. Ms. LeVault reflected, "Bundles impacted the strength of the communication in our school. Expectations, schedules, development, and morale were made congruous. And as a teacher, the centralized configuration of information was an appreciated time saver."[8] Other staff members shared similar perceptions about these weekly communication pages. Teacher-leader Talithia Palmer noted the following:

> Barb's Bundles were always informative, but *more* compelling and inspiring for me personally! Most, if not all, of Barb's bundles gave great advice, such as "The best classes are where the students are self-engaged in something that stretches their minds and interests . . . When we set the bar high, we soar with our students." (Always so encouraging!) Barb never let a staff member go unrecognized for "picking up tacks."[9]

Palmer added that the bundles helped to establish "a culture of acceptance; appreciation and resilience was cultivated amongst an entire school,"[10] noting the following:

She once captured *every* staff member's personality traits and exceptional teaching strategies in the class all in a bundle. This showed a leader who was hands on and invested in her staff . . . and actually *knew* her staff. I always looked forward to Barb's Bundles. I walked away knowing that my leader had full confidence in me as a teacher and a leader.[11]

Ashley Almonte Lopez's recollection about the bundles included the following:

Barb's Bundles provided us weekly insight as to what was going on within the school, including the projects teachers were working on, progress that was being made, general reminders, and food for thought. The bundles served as a way to keep teachers reflectively thinking about the education environment that surrounded them and also as a way for Barb to build rapport with her faculty and staff.[12]

Toward the end of the school year, each member of the school leadership team was asked to write a bundle as well. The dean of special education, Stevonna Miles Cordova, shared her challenge of writing a bundle for her colleagues:

I liked how you named it Barb's Bundles instead of weekly newsletters or something similar. You had a way of personalizing everything, which I thought was very effective in making the small school feel like a community. I will admit that I did *not* like having to create my own bundle. You are a tough act to follow, so I found trying to be witty and informative simultaneously challenging for me.[13]

At the Sterling Hall School in Toronto, the vice principal wrote a weekly information page that included humorous activities captured throughout the week. The staff enjoyed looking for who might have been highlighted that week in good fun. Weekly communications can be digital or in paper form for future reference. Teachers may choose to include certain memos that relate to their work or interest in their professional portfolios.

CUSTOMIZED WEEKLY COACHING SUPPORT

When schools enlist the support of instructional coaches, teachers can be supported through customized professional growth experiences. Coaches can share experiences and discuss teaching relative to set standards during professional conversations. Some may take on mentor roles, listening with empathy, reserving judgment, and being present more in a collegial capacity. Other coaches may be charged with the responsibility of moving teachers to exhibit more specific and informed teaching practices. Some coaches do both.

Coaches typically are teacher-leaders who have demonstrated a high degree of expertise in their teaching career. They tend to observe mentee classes and, in some cases, do demo classes to help introduce new approaches and implement how new school initiatives can take shape within the context of the classroom. Both mentors and mentees grow professionally when such collaborative roles are ingrained in a school's operation.

The idea of infusing the coaching role with weekly team-planning and team-teaching experiences had demonstrated significant merit when it was introduced at the performing arts school in Washington, DC. Teacher-leaders in the arts, primary education, math, science, and English language arts, were given a half-day teaching load in return for supporting five or more colleagues. Once a week the mentor teacher would meet for one hour to team-plan with each mentee teacher, which was followed up the next day with team-teaching an hour-long class in the context of the classroom.

The mentee teacher had an extra set of hands—as did the students—on a weekly basis. The planning conversations began by reflecting on the class from the week before, as well as the mentee sharing of the overview of highlights of the class activities when the mentor was not present. This regular and customized professional learning opportunity provided shared teaching experiences, similar to an apprenticeship model. When the mentee teachers could work alongside expert teachers, they were able to engage not only in "legitimate peripheral participation"[14] but legitimate co-teaching participation.

Reflecting on the experience a decade later, mentee Audrey LeVault shared the following:

> Ms. Nugent has been helpful . . . She showed me a review activity she did with the sixth grade; it inspired a challenging and exciting review for my students. We recently completed professional development together; we have now been talking about some of the ideas and how they have worked in our classrooms. And she shows me she values my input and ideas by asking me questions and for my opinion. When we review my lesson plans, she has good questions to add and sometimes a lower or higher differentiation idea.[15]

Restructuring schools to make room for seasoned teachers to be instructional teachers for a half-day, while providing mentorship experiences for the other part of the school day, would help support new teachers, at the same time as making seasoned teachers feel more fulfilled. Different from the current model where school administrators and coaches do not have direct instructional roles with students, such a model of part-time mentorship and a part-time classroom role would mean that teaching talent can still impact students directly.

MONTHLY EARLY DISMISSALS

It is difficult to make room for substantial interaction or response to new initiatives in a piecemeal fashion. When schools allot one class period per week for grade-level meetings, it is not enough time for teachers to share what they are doing, relay concerns about individuals who may require specialized support, or coplan any coordinated integrated or interdisciplinary activity.

Rather than teachers opting for four separate "45-minute" periods/month, it can be more productive to plan for monthly early dismissals from regular school programming. Students would not be dismissed to go home early, but rather take part in special workshops supervised by instructors from various community groups such as 4H, chess, leadership training, babysitting certification, cooking classes, and a host of cocurricular offerings, depending on the rich assortment of resources in the community.

Changing the distribution of time can lead to enhancing professional growth opportunities. Rather than weekly grade meetings, it makes sense to plan monthly early dismissals from regular programming, so that grade-level meetings can have upwards of three hours for quality professional conversation and planning action. The idea of grade meetings are designed with good intentions, but the implementation with such time limits on a weekly basis, do not, in many situations lead to meaningful change and improvement.

END-OF-YEAR PD

At the Sterling Hall School, the staff took part in a "2 by 4 conference," which involved each teacher sharing what they learned from the workshops they attended outside the school throughout the school year. The conference was set up as a "to the teachers, by the teachers, for the teachers" format. In this way, more teachers could benefit from the ideas, even if they could not attend the original conferences.

Teachers developed their leadership skills, synthesized their experiences, and had a larger audience to consider how the ideas might work or be adapted in the context of the school. As Blecher noted: "Teachers are able to be instructors and sharers in their own schools. It shouldn't be shunned to share with your peers. That's not showing off! That is helping and supporting educators and education and students, too."[16]

Fun awards at the end of a school year can also help build team spirit in a school. Certificates, trophies, plaques, or envelopes with thank-you cards are sometimes part of staff recognition systems. To honor loyalty of staff members who stay for periods of 5, 10, 15, or 20 plus years, some schools give out special envelopes with added bonus checks for seasoned professionals. At one school, the principal awarded every staff member with a banana or mini cucumber decorated with stickers—highlighting each unique contribution to the school!

TEACHER EXCHANGES

While not as commonplace as informed practice might recommend, teacher exchanges can be powerful incentives and learning opportunities. Districts, states, provinces, and countries can plan for teachers to change places to learn from and with other school cultures.

Finding out what other school cultures are like can be rewarding for the individual teacher and the system the teacher returns to. Michael Lawrence (from Australia) wrote a book about his experiences in Finland. In *Testing 3-2-1: What Australian Education Can Learn From Finland*, he describes, in sharp contrast to Australia, that most teachers in Finland find the profession fulfilling; their society respects teaching as a profession, much more so than many Western cultures.[17]

Exchanges could also happen between school districts, as well as provinces and states. It is more work to coordinate such practices to ensure smooth transitions between different institutions, but it is also important to make room for new ideas that are brought back to the home school to influence strategic planning and school-improvement efforts. The experience should not be about finding out how to replicate another school culture; rather, the sharing of each culture can be beneficial and serve as a way to share and adapt new ideas for consideration.

A culture of learning for students can happen in concert with a robust professional learning culture for a school staff. Teachers who can learn with their colleagues will be more committed to the profession. Removing the obstacles and fine-tuning how professional growth opportunities can be implemented in schools can play a key role in sustaining a fulfilled teaching workforce.

CHALLENGE CHAT

- Does mentoring or coaching happen in your school or district? Discuss.
- How comfortable do you think teachers might be in a team-teaching situation?
- What would be the barriers to coordinating a regular team-teaching approach to individualized professional learning?
- Where might be interesting places for teachers to do an exchange?

- Who could support the practice of team teaching, and what could they actually do to demonstrate that support?

NOTES

1. Pillow, A. (2021, July 26). We all hate professional development but some of y'all need it. *Edpost.* https://www.edpost.com/stories/we-all-hate-professional-development-but-some-of-yall-need-it
2. Pillow, We all hate professional development.
3. Fullan, M. (2007, Summer). Change the terms for teacher learning. *National Staff Development Council, 28*(3), 35–36. http://michaelfullan.ca/wp-content/uploads/2016/06/13396074650.pdf
4. Dewey, J. (1907). *The school and society.* Chicago, Illinois: University of Chicago Press.
5. (A. Almonte, email personal communication, June 3, 2015).
6. Alamonte, email personal communication.
7. Alamonte, email personal communication.
8. (A. LeVault, email personal communication, March 13, 2016).
9. (T. Palmer, email personal communication, March 16, 2016).
10. Palmer, email personal communication.
11. Palmer, email personal communication.
12. Almonte, email personal communication.
13. (S. Miles-Cordova, email personal communication, March 14, 2016).
14. Lave & Wenger, Situated learning.
15. LeVault, email personal communication.
16. (H. Blecher, email personal communication, July 17, 2022).
17. Lawrence, M. (2020). *Testing 3-2-1: What Australian education can learn from Finland?* Melbourne VIC, Australia: Melbourne Books.

Chapter 6

Reducing the Volume of Expectations

> *Aspirational school leaders tend to use their teaching staff to try out new ideas and set new goals for the school without considering the workload and mental load on their teaching staff—my suggestion is they should only be allowed to introduce one new process a term to allow progress without overloading them.*[1]
>
> —Dan Robinson, primary school teacher

The principal in a school tends to be that cushion between the shooting stars of initiatives and what is expected from teachers in the classroom. The unrealistic workload of teachers must be addressed if schools expect their teachers to implement the best practices. The alarming response to the National Teacher's Union survey in the United Kingdom is serious: "Teachers said their heavy workload was a significant factor in their decision to leave. More than half of the respondents (52%) said the workload was 'unmanageable' or 'unmanageable most of the time,' up from 35% in 2021."[2]

The makers of standards have failed to select which objectives are essential and which expectations are secondary or subordinate. Teachers need to be involved in selecting which expectations are essential for all students to master. Time for vertical team planning at the school level, the level closest to the student, must be built into the school schedule design, and (as mentioned in chapter 5) 45 minutes, once a week, will not lead to meaningful engagement.

The amount of content presented as curriculum in many national-, state-, and district-level documents needs a complete overhaul. The perspectives of many curriculum developers have become so entrenched with the idea that more evidence is more rigorous and that more words, pages, and prescriptions, especially material housed in elegant prose with glossy packaging, will lead to a utopia of learning. It does appear that after decades of following such assumptions, students and teachers are not better off for such unproductive efforts.

The declogging of curriculum will make room for teacher fulfillment that comes with the renewed satisfaction of meeting the needs of their learners in their classrooms. Changing the course from a ranking direction to a mastery direction requires curriculum designers to determine what is essential, what learning builds a foundation for future learning, and what experiences can shape and support future experiences.

One elementary teacher noted that the school and academic leaders worked with vertical teams of teachers to do the following:

> To develop a list of essential skills for each grade level, which then translated to the development of a new report card. Rather than a broad report card with a letter grade for the core subjects, this report card broke down the subjects and provided a detailed report on what skills each student had mastered and which they were still working on. This method provided everyone a better idea of the child's academic and social emotional development.[3]

Based on the Common Core State Standards (CCSS) at the time, one vertical team of math teachers from primary to eighth grade developed the following lists of essential skills and understandings presented in Tables 6.1, 6.2, and 6.3.

The same type of planning for what's essential can be developed for high school. For instance, Tables 6.4 and 6.5 represent sample English language arts curriculum based on adapting an ELA curriculum originally designed for the JRLA high school[4] in Detroit, Michigan, when the school first opened. Each of the 10 essential groupings was used as a base for developing the WEDJ School Pre-K–eighth grade ELA curriculum, similar to the format of the math shared in Tables 6.1, 6.2, and 6.3.

If teachers can be trusted to teach such material, then they should be encouraged to determine the essential expectations to be mastered by all students. Just because there are fewer expectations for each grade does not mean that the subject matter is any less rigorous. The choice of an essential expectation needs to be determined by a vertical team so that the understandings of a range of grade teachers can be integrated into what is reasonable for all students to master and what skills and understanding build on the mastery from the grade before.

Reeves claimed the following:

> Since the dawn of the standards movement, bitter controversies have divided educators, leaders, and policy makers about standards. But there is one issue on which everyone agrees—there are too many standards and not enough time to

Table 6.1: WEDJ School Math Essential Skills and Understandings (Pre-K to Second Grade)

Pre-K	Kindergarten	First Grade	Second Grade
Counts and prints forward and backward to 10	Counts forward and backward to 25	Prints, uses place value and count by 2, 5, and 10 to 100, counts using ordinals (1st–25th)	Prints, uses place value and count to 999, identifies ordinals that correspond from 1 to 100
Explains and shows "some" and "most"	Makes number sentences to show addition and subtraction of single digit numbers to 5	Makes number sentences to show addition and subtraction of one- and two-digit numbers to 25	Adds and subtracts two digits with regrouping
Identifies spheres in real-world objects	Identifies cubes in real-world objects	Identifies rectangular prisms in real-world objects	Identifies and sorts edges, sides, and corners of 2D figures, with an emphasis on triangles
Shows relationships between lines, circles	Shows relationships between lines, squares, rectangles	Shows relationships between lines, squares, rectangles, rectangular prisms, and cubes	Identifies and sorts edges, sides, and corners of 3D objects with an emphasis on triangular prisms
Measures length of objects comparing nonstandard measures with inches	Compares inch and feet measurements to describe width and height of objects	Compares inch and feet measurements to describe distance and height of objects	Calculates and compares perimeter and distance in terms of inches, feet, and mile measures
Tallies and uses pictorial graph to show data	Records and interprets ongoing weather chart and graph	Uses a graph to compare mass of objects	Creates survey, collects data, and displays data in a table
Sorts 2D and 3D shapes and objects	Extends a pattern based on shape, quantity, and color	Creates opposite patterns based on shape, quantity, and color	Creates symmetrical patterns using numbers and shapes
Understands difference between whole and parts	Explains the concept of one-half using manipulatives and tables	Explains the concept of one-quarter using manipulatives and tables	Demonstrates how bills and change relate to whole numbers and numerators and denominators
Tells time to the hour	Tells time to the half-hour	Tells time to the quarter-hour	Tells time to the nearest 5 minutes
Interprets situations using will/might	Uses "hottest," "warmest," "coolest," "coldest," and "above and below" to compare	Estimates heavier and lighter and compares with scale readings	Rounds whole numbers (by 10) to 100

Source: Smith, B. J. (2013). WEDJ school math essential skills and understandings (grades pre-K to 2nd grade). WEDJ School Curriculum. Washington, DC.

Table 6.2: WEDJ School Math Essential Skills and Understandings (Third to Fifth Grade)

	Third Grade	Fourth Grade	Fifth Grade
A. Number Know-How	Uses place value and notation from 0 to 1 million	Uses place value and notation from 1 million to .01 or 1/100	Uses place value and notation from 1 million to .001 or 1/1000
B. Problem/Formula Solving	Multiplies and divides single-digit numbers	Multiplies and divides up to 144 with emphasis on factoring	Multiplies and divides two-digit numbers with an emphasis on differences between multiples and factors
C. 2D Geometry	Identifies and constructs bilateral symmetry in 2D figures	Constructs parallel and intersecting lines	Measures and constructs angles
D. 3D Geometry	Constructs cubes using squares	Constructs rectangular prisms using rectangles	Constructs 3D objects using triangles
E. Measure	Chooses and applies units for linear measurement from inches, feet, and miles	Compares standard American measures with empirical measures	Converts standard American measures with empirical measures
F. Collect, Manage, and Display Data	Constructs frequency tables with a focus on identifying the median	Constructs stem-and-leaf plot graphs with a focus on identifying median and mode	Constructs line graphs and pie to illustrate mean, median, and mode
G. Patterns	Identifies patterns using edges, sides, and corners of 2D figures (to octagon)	Identifies patterns using edges, sides, and corners of 3D objects	Examines surface area patterns in nets and objects
H. Fractal Math	Adds and subtracts part numbers (decimals, same denominator fractions, money to $100)	Reduces fractions and changes between mixed fractions, improper fractions, and decimals	Adds and subtracts fractions with unlike denominators
I. Time	Tells time to the minute	Converts time zones, explains time scales (geological, eras, periods, years, decades, centuries, millenniums)	Adds and subtracts time
J. Estimation/Probability	Rounds whole numbers to the 10s and 100s	Rounds part numbers to 1 or 0	Estimates and compares standard American with empirical measures

Source: Smith, B. J. (2013). WEDJ school math essential skills and understandings (3rd to 5th grade). WEDJ School Curriculum. Washington, DC.

Table 6.3: WEDJ School Math Essential Skills and Understandings (Sixth to Eighth Grade)

	Sixth Grade	Seventh Grade	Eighth Grade
A. Number Know-How	Uses place value to identify integer measures	Uses place value to identify - and + powers	Expresses positive and negative basis
B. Problem/ Formula Solving	Calculates exponents; adds and subtracts integers with simple, one-step algebra; solves multistep problems using PEMDAS with addition and subtraction in pre-algebra	Calculates squares, square roots; solves problems using PEMDAS with all operations; algorithms with ñ, and powers	Calculates positive and negative square roots, solves proportion/ratio using formulas and first- and second-order equations
C. 2D Geometry	Classifies angles as complementary and supplementary, applies tests of congruency	Uses geometric rules to solve for missing angles; Pythagorean theorem to determine measurements	Builds elementary proofs
D. 3D Geometry	Calculates area of triangle and volume of triangular prism	Describes volume and surface area of 3D solids and relationships between curved lines, circles and spheres, and cones and pyramids	Sorts quadrilaterals by geometric properties involving diagonals
E. Measure	Calculates and uses circumference measures	Calculates coordinates using ordered pairs of integers	Charts changes in navigational course with ordered pairs and geometric formulae
F. Collect/ Manage/ Display Data	Uses technology to design graphs and tables to illustrate mean, median, mode, and range	Constructs combined graphs with two vertical axes	Solves systems using geometric axioms
G. Patterns	Reflects, translates, and rotates figures	Creates patterns using tessellations	Compares and analyzes area and volume of 2D and 3D
H. Fractal Math	Identifies relationships and can convert between percent, fractions, ratio, and decimals	Calculates rates of increase (tax, stocks)	Analyzes change in rates, mean, and percentage
I. Time	Calculates variable rates (dollars/hour)	Calculates speed as a relationship between distance and time; analyzes rates of acceleration	Finds slope and uses graphing functions
J. Estimation/ Probability	Estimates and calculates tax	Examines Fibonacci patterns in nature and other real-world phenomena	Compares and interrelates visual forms using Euclidean and non-Euclidean rules

Source: Smith, B. J. (2013). WEDJ school math essential skills and understandings (6th to 8th grade). WEDJ School Curriculum. Washington, DC.

Table 6.4: Sample Grade 8 Through 12 ELA Expectations

Essential Thread	Grade 8 (diagnostic)	Grade 10	Grade 12
Apply—Use expanded word choice for enhancing meaning.	Use thesaurus to eliminate repetition in writing.	Examine meaning of uncommon words and most commonly misspelled words.	Identify and select the most appropriate word meaning and figurative language (fiction) for reading and writing.
Respond—Respond verbally using phrasing that identifies key ideas and details.	Identify and discuss story elements in a novel, as well as features of different nonfiction books.	Identify features of mixed genres in novels and patterns within legal documents (i.e., contracts).	Provide evidence in verbal form that analyzes and compares text features and ideas in two novels, two poems, and two media sources.
Sequence—Sequence ideas in a logical manner.	Write a recipe for completing a task in a logical order.	Put a story and nonfictional text in a logical order.	Organize a sequence of images and texts that identify key events in a novel, manual, and business plan.
Write—Write expository texts.	Plan, draft, edit, and write 3-paragraph expository summaries about fiction and nonfiction texts.	Plan, draft, edit, and write 5-paragraph expository articles about fiction and nonfiction texts.	Plan, draft, edit, and write expository essays about fiction and nonfiction texts.
Use—Use technology as a tool to enhance learning.	Revise targeted manipulation in text and media (explicit/implicit) messages.	Make use of design elements (font, style, inserts) for emphasis in writing nonfiction or about fictional texts.	Use technology to enhance understanding of fiction and nonfiction texts and media sources.
Generate—Generate thoughtful and insightful questions that address perspective and inference.	Use ideas from different cultures to generate questions about fiction and nonfiction texts.	Use ideas from different historical periods to generate questions about fiction and nonfiction texts.	Ask questions that reveal capacity to make inferences to account for missing information in fiction and nonfiction texts.
Write—Write persuasive texts.	Write a 3-paragraph formal business letter persuading someone to hire you.	Write a 5-paragraph essay about different points of view in a variety of texts.	Write a persuasive argument for a letter to an editor of a media source.
Create—Create a written response to a text using key ideas and details.	Identify key features in a fictional short story and a nonfiction article.	Write the next chapter of a fiction or nonfiction book.	Provide evidence in written form that analyzes and compares key features of two novels and two documents.
Write—Write narrative texts.	Display awareness of self through journal writing—traits both positive and negative.	Write a biography of someone life.	Write an autobiography based on regular journal goal-setting entries.
Polish—Polish written and media works to communicate with precision and accuracy.	Evaluate and revise texts with improper grammar and spelling.	Use a variety of sentence starters and types of sentences in writing.	Use accurate grammatical syntax and spelling in written and spoken language with reference to fictional and nonfiction text.

cover them . . . The only reasonable way to address these challenges is the use of Power Standards (. . . such as Priority Standards, Essential Standards, etc.).[5]

Dabbling with a tsunami of random content has not made the art of teaching doable, manageable, or rewarding, nor has it contributed to cultivating a larger critical mass of young minds capable of solving tomorrow's problems.

By identifying fewer, more rigorous expectations, the teacher can concentrate more time and be able to apply more habits of mind and multi-intelligences within lessons as well as build out authentic and engaging project-based learning activities to make the learning stick. Additionally, by reducing the number of power standards or essential skills, especially in mathematics and English language arts, there can be more room for other learning experiences in the form of electives and microcredentials, which often are cut due to time restrictions in the overall school year.

How many disconnected math worksheets need to be completed for homework or to fill the minutes of class time before educators realize that a curriculum needs to be more than dots on a Jackson Pollock painting? How many questions at the end of each chapter of a novel must students answer—and teachers review—before a culture realizes that busy work will not amount to a meaningful education? If education is moving beyond its present course, it will need to declutter the volume of expectations to make it more manageable and motivating.

There seems to be two steps missing in the design of curriculum. When all the standards are listed in government or school documents, they have not been vetted for the degree of replication in many grades. Yes, review has its place, but not in determining what should be distinct or unique to each grade. Second, once the synthesis and determination of what is essential (that which is unique and progresses and builds on concepts from the prior grade), there are few samples of how such material can be coordinated as project-based curriculum resources.

One English language arts teacher described the value of working hand in hand with school leaders "to develop project-based curriculum packets that helped the students comprehend and analyze the novels in an exciting and authentic manner."[6] Teachers can bring the context of the school and the community to the curriculum resources when they are encouraged to design curriculum materials.

A further problem worthy of mention is the assumption that curriculum materials are a panacea "fix." Many schools pilot initiatives for the purpose of fine-tuning programs to launch on a large scale, often missing the point or value of localized and community-based contexts. Apart from being bombarded with new initiatives to try out, it is often a perception that the feedback from teachers in various pilots is rarely addressed when the initiatives may

Table 6.5: Sample Grade 12 ELA Expectations in Two Semesters

Essential Thread	Grade 12 Fiction Essential Skills/ Understandings	Purpose Projects— Fiction	Grade 12 Nonfiction Essential Skills/ Understandings	Purpose Projects— Nonfiction
Apply—Use expanded word choice for enhancing meaning.	Identify and select the most appropriate word meaning and figurative language for reading and writing fiction.	Poetry Audit Author Review ACT Test	Identify and select the most appropriate word meaning for reading and writing nonfiction.	Manual Maker; Business Plan
Respond—Respond verbally using phrasing that identifies key ideas and details.	Provide evidence in verbal form that analyzes and compares text features in two novels and two poems.	Poetry Audit; Author Review	Provide evidence in verbal form that analyzes and compares text features and ideas in two media sources.	Media Appraisal
Sequence—Sequence ideas in a logical manner.	Create a sequence of images and texts that identify key events in a novel.	Storyboard	Organize a sequence of images and texts that identify key events in a manual and business plan.	Manual Maker; Business Plan
Write—Write expository texts.	Plan, draft, edit, and write expository texts about fiction.	Author Review	Plan, draft, edit, and write expository nonfiction texts.	Manual Maker; Business Plan
Use—Use technology as a tool to enhance learning.	Use technology to enhance understanding of fiction texts.	Poetry Audit; Storyboard; Author Review	Use technology to enhance understanding of non-fiction texts and media sources.	Media Appraisal
Generate—Generate thoughtful and insightful questions that address perspective and inference.	Ask questions that make inferences to account for missing information in fiction texts.	Poetry Audit; Author Review	Ask questions that reveal the capacity to make inferences to account for missing information in nonfiction texts.	Media Appraisal

Essential Thread	Grade 12 Fiction Essential Skills/ Understandings	Purpose Projects— Fiction	Grade 12 Nonfiction Essential Skills/ Understandings	Purpose Projects— Nonfiction
Write—Write persuasive texts.	Write a persuasive argument about the value in reading a fictional book or series.		Write a persuasive argument for a letter to an editor of a media source.	Editorial Writer
Create—Create written response to text using key ideas and details	Provide evidence in written form that analyzes and compares key features of two novels.	Storyboard; Author Review	Provide evidence in written form that analyzes and compares key features of two documents.	Manual Maker
Write—Write narrative texts.	Write a narrative text as a historical fiction as a screenplay.		Write an autobiography based on regular journal goal-setting entries.	Life Story
Polish—Polish written and media works to communicate with precision and accuracy.	Use accurate grammatical syntax and spelling in written and spoken language with reference to fictional text.	Author Review	Use accurate grammatical syntax and spelling in written and spoken language with reference to nonfiction text.	Manual Maker; Business Plan; Media Appraisal; Editorial Writer's Life Story

or may not be revised. The top-down development of materials takes away teacher ownership and buy-in.

The notion that all that is needed lies within a textbook or planning guide generated from a central office is pale in comparison to what teachers can own and design when given ample time for resource development. Just as students are proud of their creative work, imagine what a school system would be like if all students could be taught by teachers who had developed their own teaching programs! Teachers are much more than waiters serving someone else's meal. If we want students to be inventors and innovators, then teachers need to be in the thick of idea generation too.

CHALLENGE CHAT

- How much time each day do you think teachers need to plan and develop curriculum materials?
- Do you work in a school or district where vertical teams of teachers establish essential skills or power standards?
- What would be the challenges involved in customizing a report card to address essential skills established by teachers?
- We can replicate the densely prosed curriculum of yesterday, or we can look for new ways to generate ownership and empowerment over teaching and learning. Discuss the following quote by Charles F. Kettering with respect to your thoughts for next steps for school curriculum design: "You can't have a better tomorrow if you are thinking about yesterday all the time."[7]

NOTES

1. Robinson, D. (2022, March). *Aspirational school leaders tend to use their teaching staff to try out new ideas and set new goals for the*. [Post]. LinkedIn. https://www.linkedin.com/in/daniel-robinson-teacher/recent-activity/

2. PA Media. (2022, April 11). 44% of teachers in England plan to quit within five years. *The Guardian.* https://www.theguardian.com/education/2022/apr/11/teachers-england-plan-to-quit-workloads-stress-trust

3. (A. Almonte, email personal communication, June 3, 2015).

4. Smith, B. J. (2011). ELA curriculum. Jalen Rose Leadership Academy (JRLA). Detroit, Michigan.

5. Reeves, D. (2019, July 14). Too many standards—too little time. *Creative Leadership Solutions*. https://www.creativeleadership.net/blog/too-many-standards-too-little-time

6. Almonte, email personal communication.

7. Kettering. C. F. (2023). Quotes in Goodreads. https://www.goodreads.com/quotes/887691-you-can-t-have-a-better-tomorrow-if-you-are-thinking

Chapter 7

Trusting Teachers' Capacities to Assess Students

With the evolution and ever-increasing frequency and sense of competition that comes with these standardized tests, it's no wonder that teachers are becoming frustrated and leaving altogether.[1]

—Lexi Ramirez

Teachers are seated next to learners every day. They know best what students know and what they do not know. Standardized tests are often presented as a fair, objective way to find out what students know. A fair test, however, is one where students have been taught all that they have been tested on. In order to gain supposedly norm-referenced deviations in results, test makers need to include content that many students have not been exposed to. It can be frustrating for teachers when their teaching is driven by a moving target.

Teachers can test what has been taught; they are in a better position to design tests that address what has been taught in their classrooms. The business of standardized testing has undermined the trust many institutions used to place in their teachers. Even more disappointing is that many educators have also bought into the distorted concern that when grades are left to teachers, they will be inflated—as if some percentage score was the only accurate measure of what students know.

It is time to remove the weeds of standardized test practice, which not only wastes opportunities for teachers to customize lessons for their students, but it takes away from the time needed for students to apply their understandings in project work, service learning, or internships experiences. Standardized assessments do not measure the kind of higher-level thinking our students will need to participate in their complex futures.

The interrupting presence of the practice tests and the unproven worth of these annual tests, often given to students as young as those in grade one, is in direct conflict with peer-reviewed research in education and grounded pedagogic curriculum. Yet in many countries, misguided assumptions that such testing is true grounds for comparison is commonplace.

It is time to recognize that the annual use and worshipping of such tests is a waste of precious time and probably a key force in cultivating student and teacher disengagement. Letting standardized assessment drive the direction and vision for a school only serves to clog the minds of students and teachers, further distancing all community members in an educational system from reaching the goal of building a civil and knowing society.

The gap in education between engagement and learning is the gap that should not be ignored. There is no qualitative metric that addresses the level of engagement as a variable in standardized test results. The assumption that all students who take these tests have the same engagement levels in their classrooms and/or on the test is naïve.

The research about school engagement has consistently been riding a parallel wave, painting a picture that too many students are not engaged after grade five, and yet the gatekeepers of the standardized test movement seem to ignore this data altogether. If schools are committed to quality improvement, how can they possibly rely on the questionable narrow results of quantitative testing?

Diagnostic tests used and designed by teachers in advance of a unit have far more potential to influence learning. Students who demonstrate the capacity to meet the expectations can move on to an enriched study, while others who need the time to learn can continue with the planned program of study. Students are disengaged when they are bored or when they feel the pace of teaching moves too quickly, not allowing the time to grapple with, grasp, and apply their understandings. School leaders need to make room and provide supports for teachers to engage all students in their classrooms.

Teachers are taught to teach all the students, so the notion of mastery is ingrained in their DNA. They are also taught about the idea of an artificial bell curve, which accepts a culture that some students will know more than others, a culture where it is commonplace to distribute the knowns from the unknowing. It doesn't make sense to have elaborate point scores for grades or standardized test scores if the goal of education is to teach all students.

Teachers know who needs more and differentiated supports in their classrooms. They also know which students have mastered the expectations of what is needed to know to apply their understandings in the real world. There is little doubt teachers can replicate their assessments of students when the terms are fair.

Pass-or-fail assessments, or assessments with fewer qualifiers, not only reduce the overengineered burden on the teacher to rank students on four or more degrees on basically arbitrary scales, but such conditions produce more just results. When more teachers can come up with the same result for the same quality of work and understanding, then students and teachers are assessing on a fairer-learning ground. This in contrast to the busywork of a competitive field that does more to increase disengagement and lack of respect for the institution of school.

Imagine the time saved if a teacher had to use more simplified and elegant scales of assessment. In the book *Assessment Tools and Systems*, this argument is further explored. This example from the book (Tables 7.1[2] and 7.2[3]) reveals that assessment tools can be revised with more precision paid to the criteria and expectations, as opposed to the misguided attention often paid to assessing the degrees of not meeting requirements in the forms of Cs, Ds, or Fs.

Table 7.2 reduces the volume of text for teachers to read but clarifies which specific criteria students need to work on. Clearly designed assessment tools can function as instructional tools when students can look through the lens of the tool to self-assess their work. Rubrics should not be overused either;

Table 7.1: Sample Writing Rubric from Thoughtco.com

Areas of Assessment	A	B	C	D
Ideas	Presents ideas in an original manner.	Presents ideas in a consistent manner.	Ideas are too general.	Ideas are vague or unclear.
Organization	Strong and organized beginning/middle/end.	Organized beginning/middle/end.	Some organization; attempts at a beginning/middle/end.	No organization; lacks beginning/middle/end.
Understanding	Writing shows strong understanding.	Writing shows a clear understanding.	Writing shows adequate understanding.	Writing shows little understanding.
Word Choice	Sophisticated use of nouns and verbs makes the essay very informative.	Nouns and verbs make essay informative.	Needs more nouns and verbs.	Little or no use of nouns and verbs.
Sentence Structure	Sentence structure enhances meaning; flows throughout the piece.	Sentence structure is evident; sentences mostly flow.	Sentence structure is limited; sentences need to flow.	No sense of sentence structure or flow.
Mechanics	Few (if any) errors.	Few errors.	Several errors.	Numerous errors.

Table 7.2: Sample Interactive Writing Rubric

Self-Review	2 = excellent level of evidence, 1 = some evidence, NY = not yet	Teacher Review
	Ideas presented in a logical manner (a nice flow).	
	Ideas include solid details.	
	Ideas include original creative thought.	
	Strong and organized beginning paragraph.	
	Captivating starter sentence.	
	Strong and organized middle paragraphs.	
	Strong and organized ending paragraph.	
	Inspiring/memorable ending sentence.	
	Use of sophisticated nouns.	
	Use of sophisticated verbs.	
	Use of words and/or punctuation to transition sentences smoothly.	
	Use of a variety of sentence types for emphasis.	
	Accurate grammar.	
	Accurate spelling.	
	Accurate punctuation.	
/30 points	Scores (Mastery equals 48 points or greater)	/30 points
Comments:		

finding a balance of quality assessments can give students ample feedback for celebrating and improving their work.

The use of more interactive rubrics, for instance, can increase the student onus for learning, reducing the drain on teachers to find time to reteach lessons. Additionally, making the work of assessment manageable can minimize the frustration for teachers compelled to move on while knowing student learning, for some, has been left behind.

It is time for many school decision-makers to understand how standardized tests and commercial assessments are taking too much precedence over teaching and learning, as well as how such a narrow view of success is contributing to diminished educational returns. Mastery rather than ranking approaches to learning puts the trust back in teachers' hands—the people closest to assess the depth and breadth of student learning.

Systems have tried the standardized ranking approach to schooling for decades with little or no evidence of improvement. Teachers must play a fundamental role in education. They cannot simply be technicians who paint by numbers. Rather, they are highly skilled professionals capable of determining how well students are learning and what they need to do to support all learners. Ranking students does not require teachers to help all students learn.

School leaders who expect teachers to move on after each lesson accept a distorted view that ranking is normal, and schooled cultures can permit students to fail. This can't be engaging for teachers or students.

CHALLENGE CHAT

1. It has been said that ranking interferes with mastery. What do you think?
2. Should failure be a part of formative and summative assessment? Discuss.
3. Do you believe teachers have the capacity to assess their students better than standardized tests? Explain.
4. Classroom assessment tools can guide instruction if they are clear and easy to follow. Your thoughts?
5. Diagnostic testing can be an important step in determining what to teach students. Why do you think this form of assessment is rarely employed?
6. What would happen if standardized tests were given only in grades 7 and 10? Would the education system fall apart? Would student engagement in learning improve?

NOTES

1. Lexi Ramirez (2020, March 5). *Why teachers are saying goodbye.* [Post]. LinkedIn. https://www.linkedin.com/pulse/why-teachers-saying-goodbye-lexi-evans/?trackingId=HBk6xADMU0JL%2BVj2SBH2gA%3D%3D.

2. Smith, B. J. (2023). *Assessment tools and systems: Meaningful feedback approaches to promote critical and creative thinking.* Lanham, Maryland: Rowman & Littlefield.

3. Smith, *Assessment tools and systems.*

Chapter 8

Respect and Recognition of Teacher Insight, Action, and Creativity

> *Honor them: Acknowledge the good things happening in their classroom, as well as their efforts outside the classroom (if they maintain a blog, classwork of their own, completed a degree or certificate, have been through something big personally but show up every day to work and give to their students with their hearts).*[1]
>
> —Maria T. McCabe, educator, Krakow

While teachers thrive in creative environments, they also need to be respected for their insight and courageous actions. When teachers are given instructional prescriptions and expected to be on the same page at the same time as other teachers—such expectations run counter to the laws of nature. Just as students are unique, require choice, and are engaged by meaningful activity, so too are teachers. For early childhood educator Lori Fuchs from Pittsburgh, Pennsylvania, it all boils down to *respect*:

> Respect from communities for what we do, we love these children and want the best from them. Respect from other professionals, we too have educations, we too work hard, we too work more than 40 hours a week, we too are professionals. Respect from leadership for what we have to offer, what we have to give to the school, the students, the community. Respect from each other, we are all traveling the same path but are walking in different footsteps. Respect from students, we are trying but often have our hands tied. Respect.[2]

It may seem simple for some teachers to follow a table of contents in a textbook or an artificially inseminated pacing guide; however, having a syllabus designed by others can suck the life out of the design-thinking part of teaching. Educators should not have others do the preparation for their teaching; it removes their humanity from the equation. Fuchs added,

> I'd be happy if we were just allowed to teach. Yes, I have standards to meet, yes, there are goals that need to be accomplished, but often the best lessons are created in the moment . . . the off-topic question that creates a fantastic learning opportunity . . . then, we are facilitators. Then we all grow. Good teachers are great teachers when you let them grow with the students and demonstrate the learning is a process of inquiry and not just a lesson in a text book.[3]

Many students are aware of when their teachers' hands are tied, fixed to a premixed curriculum. How can students or teachers be engaged when teaching is reduced to a mouthing of the words, as if performing daily in a lip-sync competition would lead to success? Teachers have much more to offer than a practice limited by robotic compliance. How can these professionals feel any sense of recognition for implementing tools created by others far removed from their classrooms?

Removing the barriers to innovation and embracing the insight and actions of teachers should help cultivate more engaging and innovative teaching and learning approaches, professional planning aimed at meeting the needs of all students in their classrooms. We must trust our teachers and provide substantial supports for them. School leaders need to recognize their worth and insight.

In her book *Teacher*, Australian author Gabbie Stroud shared her sadness about not being a teacher anymore:

> A cold sweat shivered on my skin. This is it, I thought. This isn't teaching. I'm not a teacher anymore . . . There's something sinister happening to this profession that I loved. And it breaks my heart. We don't trust our teachers anymore.[4]

There are many teachers, like Gabbie, who may not have left the building and share the frustration of being handcuffed to programming separate from themselves. They may be present in schools, but their hearts and passion for the profession have been drained by a system polishing the deck chairs on a sinking ship. Letting others do the thinking and planning for teachers has contributed to the broken relationship between the teacher and what and how they teach. Many have little say in designing curriculum, assessing students, and coordinating schedules.

Few professions are handed a script and expected to follow the directions of some artificial recipe. What one doctor or lawyer does and says in one hospital or courtroom will not be the same as what other physicians or legal representatives would say in their specific contexts. One could argue their expertise is generally respected.

In the case of teachers, however, it seems like education experts are positioned outside the classroom, as if the system demoted teachers to nonexpert roles. This may be where the rubber meets the road. If school leaders can accept that the people situated directly in the contexts of teaching and learning are not only valuable assets but experts in the field, many teachers can begin to renew their pride and fulfillment in the profession. Echoing teachers' calls to action, David Stieber noted the following:

> We want to be a part of all of this work. We have the expertise, the experience, the degrees, the certifications upon certifications. We know how schools work. This is how we can attract teachers and re-energize the experts that we do have.[5]

Walker noted that Richard Ingersoll had examined a "mountain of research" confirming that many STEM teachers are leaving public education, "not merely because the economic rewards are greater in the private sector, but because they lack the autonomy to engage their students in a creative manner."[6] Recognition and respect for the insights and action of teachers as experts is one of many conditions that needs to be addressed by school systems in order to shift the tide from apathy to enthusiasm. It is time to build positive cultures that arouse the teacher giant within.

According to Australian educator Cameron Paterson, "Fundamental transformation of the entire one-size-fits schooling model is needed to build a more potent and fulfilled profession—one in which educators are empowered as design thinkers."[7] He acknowledged how teachers as curriculum designers are key to school transformation. He added, "If we want people in classrooms teaching kids, let's press the pedal on creative possibilities, pull the reins back on the crushing bureaucracy, and trust and support teachers to be the outstanding professionals that they are."[8] Each classroom has a collection of students that is unique to that composition of individuals and how each student and the teacher relate to each other.

A textbook or curriculum guide cannot capture the distinctive culture of each community. Teachers who are supported and rewarded for redesigning lessons to meet their student needs are not only enhancing the potential for student engagement, they are creating the conditions for their own professional fulfillment. It feels good when kids learn, but it feels better when they want to learn. According to Steve Haberlin,

> When one is feeling creative, playful, and innovative, how can they feel emotionally exhausted? . . . Being dissatisfied with one's accomplishments or a loss of self-competence can also be remedied perhaps by giving back autonomy to teachers, allowing them to experiment, dabble, and create through their teaching. Creativity itself can be the reward.[9]

Haberlin recommended that district and school administrators (as well as federal and state lawmakers) who are responsible for key decisions "should take note of the significance of encouraging teachers to be creative and providing discretion and autonomy."[10] Schools that encourage creativity amongst their students, teachers, and even families demonstrate growth mindsets, open to new ideas and possibilities for making continuous improvements that are much more than words in a document.

With the abundance of standards clogging the teacher plans, there is little room for teachers to model creativity for students. The monotony of introducing lessons, handing out assignments, and checking for individuals' understanding in a classroom full of 20 or more students in a fixed time frame under an hour does not attract talent to the profession. Students are expected to demonstrate original ideas and creativity, yet with the way many schools are designed, it can be very difficult for teachers to be creative.

The recent interest in Pinterest, where many teachers share teaching materials they have developed, is evidence of the pride teachers feel about their work—so much so that they make it available for free or for a small fee for other educators. Through Pinterest and other shared social media platforms, students and teachers can benefit from artifacts shared to support teaching and learning.

The level of prescription in some how-to-teach books reaches far beyond respect. Bringing a stop watch into classes to time how long an introduction is or using the same snapping finger signal to quiet students is the antithesis of quality teaching. The assumption is that champion teachers only teach in one highly teacher-directed way ignores over half a century of solid, peer-reviewed research in curriculum, teaching, and learning. Sadly, in many low-income districts, the paint-by-numbers teaching approach has thwarted the artistry of the profession.

Educational experts who have taken the rigorous road of reading and conducting peer-reviewed research and practice are well aware that prescriptive dogmas of scripted teaching are not suitable for teachers and it is disingenuous for teachers to become complacent puppets. Experts need to challenge such directives and the funding that fuels poor teaching practices, as all children regardless of their zip or postal codes should receive a quality education. Teachers should not fear the prospect of losing their job because school leaders have taken short cuts.

There are some school leaders who have never taught in a classroom nor taken any required education courses. How can such individuals coordinate performance reviews without a solid understanding of teaching and learning?

There is an assumption that schooling is a one-size-fits all operation and that the formula for success must exist in the schools with high standardized test scores. All the school has to do is replicate what the supposedly high-test-performing school does, right? Such a perspective could not be farther from the truth. Such misguided and undergrounded assertions are dangerous for society.

Fear and the denouncement of creativity are not what teachers need to thrive and support their students. The advent of formulas and the ill-advised notion that a fixed way of schooling will be some panacea may be the food of political discourse, but it is harmful for student engagement and teacher morale. The members of each school community need to cultivate the uniqueness of their school, and when they do, they can be empowered, engaged, and fulfilled.

The people in each school must be given the freedom to be original; after all, how can the problems of tomorrow be addressed if students are only taught to memorize the solutions from the past? There is also too much control promoting sameness at school district, state/provincial, and national levels.

If creativity is a value and recognized as a serious need to cultivate within our students, school systems must embrace it by permitting teachers to model it and nurture it in their students. The risk of making mistakes is part of creativity, but the risk of not being creative can be much more detrimental in the long term. Students need role models that are not afraid to take risks, and teachers need their supervisors to accept that each teacher is not the same.

CHALLENGE CHAT

- What are ways to treat teachers with respect?
- What do you think an expert is?
- Do you know of teachers who have had an opportunity to design curriculum?
- What are the advantages and disadvantages of supporting teacher creativity?
- Should teachers have time in their schedules to create new teaching tools on their own or with others?
- What do you think of theses quotes shared by Douglas Reeves?

When I surveyed more than 6,000 teachers . . . they estimated only four percent of their decisions were autonomous or at their discretion, compared to more than seventy percent that were administratively determined, with the balance being decisions that were collaborative with their colleagues.[11]

School systems hire teachers because they are bright, creative, and independent, and then seem deeply disappointed because they turn out to be bright, creative, and independent. This is no way to treat professionals; it's no wonder they want to leave.[12]

NOTES

1. McCabe, M. T. (2022, March). *Honor them: Acknowledge the good things happening in their classroom, as well as their efforts outside the classroom (if they.* [Post]. LinkedIn. https://www.linkedin.com/in/maria-t-mccabe-75954a58/recent-activity/

2. Fuchs, L. (2022, May 13). In P. Sahlberg's *New education minister Jason Clare can fix the teacher shortage crisis but not with labor election plan. The Conversation.* https://theconversation.com/new-education-minister-jason-clare-can-fix-the-teacher-shortage-crisis-but-not-with-labors-election-plan-184321

3. Fuchs, In P. Sahlberg's New education minister.

4. Stroud, G. *Teacher.* (2018). In C. Paterson's *Who is going to teach the kids?* (2022, March 29). *Getting Smart.* https://www.gettingsmart.com/2022/03/29/who-is-going-to-teach-the-kids/

5. Stieber, D. (2022, February 14). *America's teachers aren't burned out. We are demoralized. EdSurge.* https://www.edsurge.com/news/2022-02-14-america-s-teachers-aren-t-burned-out-we-are-demoralized

6. Walker, T. (2015, August 26). Want to reduce the teacher shortage? Treat teachers like professionals (An interview with Richard Ingersoll). *NEA Today.* https://www.nea.org/advocating-for-change/new-from-nea/want-reduce-teacher-shortage-treat-teachers-professionals

7. Paterson, C. (2022, March 29). *Who is going to teach the kids? Getting Smart.* https://www.gettingsmart.com/2022/03/29/who-is-going-to-teach-the-kids/

8. Paterson, *Who is going to teach the kids?*

9. Haberlin, S. (2023). Want teacher to be happy? Let them be creative. *Education World.* https://www.educationworld.com/blog/want-teachers-be-happy-let-them-be-creative

10. Haberlin, Want teacher to be happy?

11. Reeves, D. B. (2016). *From leading to succeeding: The seven elements of effective leadership in education.* Bloomington, Indiana: Solution Tree Press.

12. Reeves, D. B. (2018, May 1). *Seven keys to restoring the teacher pipeline.* ASCD. https://www.ascd.org/el/articles/seven-keys-to-restoring-the-teacher-pipeline

Chapter 9

Teaching Supports

Q: Quick question—please share what comes to your mind first. What kinds of resources do you think would help teachers to stay in the profession?

Response: Mental health resources, which include professional development![1]

—Ghada Sadaka, school leader, York Region District School Board, Canada

Many schools provide teachers with support in many ways; more supports and new ways to help educators meeting new demands of the day are always needed. Supports can come in the form of additional staff, the restructuring of existing staff, and the provisions made for professional learning and materials. This chapter will focus on the aid that can be provided through human capital.

The use of the term *surrogate* can refer to reliable individuals that serve or support the teaching staff. There are many people who can replace a qualified teacher when required in the short term. Ideally, substitute teachers are certified teachers, but often it can be difficult to find replacements for the classroom when a teacher is ill. Teaching assistants, as well as school administrators, can also stand in for the teacher. Having a talented pool of adults ready and skilled to substitute for teachers when they are away is a key component of a solid support system.

A shortage of substitute teachers increases the stress on teachers. As Kamenetz noted, teachers are picking up slack for absent colleagues. They're covering for unfilled positions And 55% of them say they will leave teaching sooner than they had originally planned, according to a poll of its members by the nation's largest teachers union.[2]

The importance of preparation time, as mentioned in chapter 3, cannot be overstated. When teachers need to fill in for a sick colleague, they lose their time to plan, adding frustration to their day.

Many unwell teachers, who should stay at home, often come to school, not wanting to burden their colleagues. This can have a domino effect with more sick teachers, adding students to the mix as well. When school leaders cannot access qualified teacher substitutes, they often have no choice but to hire noncertified adults to supervise the students until the teacher is well enough to return to work.

Similar to many countries, Australia has a specialist teacher problem: "Almost 10% of Australian high school students will never be taught by a qualified math teacher. Experienced science teachers are also in high demand, and three out of four public schools don't have a qualified music teacher."[3]

Qualified teachers will continue to be in demand in the near future, given the talk of educators exiting the profession early. While all students should be taught by qualified teachers, some students may have specialists in a subject area who have not taken courses to be certified in education. When there are teacher shortages in some communities, principals may have little choice but to hire noncertified teachers.

Ideally, uncertified teachers would take on internship roles or teaching assistant (TA) positions where they could be working side by side in the classroom with a qualified teacher. In this way, the set of additional hands can function as more helpful hands to support the teacher and the students. Over time, school leaders can also approve further support by paying for or subsidizing course work that can lead to full teaching qualifications.

Teaching assistants, particularly in primary classrooms, can provide significant help. What teaching assistants do can vary from school to school. They should be perceived by the students as a co-teacher, sharing the teaching and the grunt part of preparing and cleaning up after lessons. The word *assistant* can imply a reduced status, but a *co-teacher* is someone who is interested in refining their teaching craft. There are school systems that do not permit TAs or co-teachers to attend professional learning workshops. This seems at odds with goals of building a critical mass of exceptional teachers.

All staff in a school should take part in a cycle of professional learning and performance review based on expectations as outlined in their job description. The feedback given to a qualified teacher might be very different from the feedback offered to a noncertified teaching assistant. A school nurse, lunchroom supervisor, and vice principal should all receive feedback and professional growth opportunities that align with their specific responsibilities.

In the United States, Teach for America (TFA) was established to urge university graduates who have not specialized in education to "sacrifice" a year or more following graduation to teach in classrooms as a way of giving back before moving on with their planned career stream. Participating in TFA also reduces student loans—an added incentive for many.

While more TFA bodies, who are usually paid less than certified teachers, are often welcomed in a school, the idea that teaching is a short-term service job (until something better comes along) is not the kind of sustained support a school needs. Mind you, in some cases, TFA teachers do decide to make teaching a long-term career.

TFA teachers who show promise and commitment to the profession should be required to set goals to meet certified standards for teaching. Rather than a pitstop, schools need to make the prospect of teaching as a life career as attractive as or more than other competing fields for young talent. Schools invest in every adult who is part of the education workforce. A high turnover of staff, regardless of qualifications, can signal waste and can prompt a depleting morale.

On the one hand, using unqualified teachers can be perceived by parents as a disadvantage, but on the other hand, schools can keep classroom sizes down with a combination of certified and noncertified teachers. When schools hire less qualified teachers, they should ensure that a customized and differentiated induction program be put in place to support both certified novice teachers and noncertified teacher supports.

At first glance, it can seem like a blessing when administrators manage their budgets to make room to hire lunchroom and recess supervisors, teaching assistants, and/or subject matter experts or individuals who take on Teach for America (TFA)–type positions. When classrooms have an excess of 20 students and the schedule of teachers is jam-packed, the more such human aids become necessary.

In California the pattern of teacher shortages has been increasing since 2012. Prior to the pandemic, many districts had to hire teachers with substandard qualifications to address the teacher shortages:

> In recent years, due to a shortage of fully qualified teachers in California, positions have increasingly been filled with underprepared teachers who have not completed the requirements for full credentials—either interns or those teaching on 1-year permits or waivers. The number of substandard credentials and permits issued in California nearly tripled from 2012–13 to 2019–20, numbering more than 13,000 annually.[4]

Parents and community volunteers can provide supervisory supports as well. In one school, parents were asked to share their talents as guest speakers in classrooms. Two parents in Virginia with a rich background in film and television production were asked to teach a film studies course for students in grades three, four, and five. The students entered their videos into a national competition and took home first prize for their work. The quality of the teaching was incredible, but a staff member needed to be present for safety and supervisory protocols.

After a rigorous morning or afternoon of teaching, it can be frustrating for a teacher to have to supervise at lunch or during other student breaks in the day. Breaks tend to provide opportunities for students to socialize, ideally in ways that apply character, leadership, and other living skills. When there is no deliberate instructional time dedicated to teaching positive personal and social qualities, then recess time can be spaces and places where bullying and other antisocial behaviors can be cultivated, thus taxing teachers even more when they are scheduled for recess duty.

While students do need a chance for unstructured play, especially in elementary school, it can be difficult to manage the supervision of such time. Small school communities tend to have fewer discipline issues. As administrators and school boards continue to increase the physical size of schools to put more students in fewer buildings, the more schools will require additional supports for noninstructional school activity.

Unlike a school bus driver who can be assigned adult assistants to manage difficult behavior, recess and lunch supervisors are often left to deal with misbehavior without adequate training on how to diffuse volatile situations in the school yard or cafeterias. It can vary from school to school with what adult-to-student ratios are used in such unstructured school time. The critical mass of students can be overwhelming for any adult to supervise. Even when teachers are assigned such support duties, they can often feel a sense of relief when the time ends without any incidents to report.

Whenever codes of conduct are broken on the bus, school yard, or lunchroom, such disruption can often spill over into the classroom, making the subject of "classroom management" a consequential invader of teaching and learning space. Furthermore, Kelly's study of 5,000 teachers and 50,000 students revealed a "strong association" between teacher burnout, student behavior, and outcomes.[5] She claimed that "students taught by teachers showing signs of burnout were more likely to exhibit disruptive behaviours and reduced motivation as well as perform less well on assessments than other students."[6]

Without addressing the real-world need for young people to build social and emotional capacity, teaching and learning will be challenged as the primary focus in a classroom. Rather than team- teaching to reduce the teacher-to-student ratio in a classroom, many assistants tend to work one-to-one with the more disruptive students.

Schools that provide student leadership opportunities have reduced the volume of behavioral issues, which collaterally can minimize the need for adult interventions on the part of teachers, teacher assistants, lunchroom supervisors, and school administrators. In one study of a school in Mississauga, Ontario, it was common to have upwards of 20 students lined up cut the vice principal's office, requiring disciplinary measures after recess. After the grade seven and eight students took part in a playground leadership development program and implemented structured play activities for the younger students, the lineups disappeared.

In such scenarios, younger students had an option to take part in structured play, emulating camp life activities (i.e., cooperative games, tag games, etc.), while the older student supervisors no longer stood around in clumps of cliques, displaying words or actions contrary to positive school cultures. The time for developing such programs needs to be part of the overall school's organization of time.

At another high school, student leaders set up a room called "the zoo," where they organized board and card games for students to opt into during prep or free time. Supervising teachers often played games with the students, supporting and modelling social and emotional skills through their wins and losses.

Teaching assistants, substitute teachers, parents, school administrators, and even students and parents can provide surrogate supports for teachers in a school. There are many ways schools can be designed to increase supports for teachers. Gathering ideas from teachers directly in the form of annual interviews and surveys can be a sound strategy for making the most out of surrogate support options. In the next chapter, a focus on mentoring will detail ways, given additional preparation time, that teachers can support each other.

CHALLENGE CHAT

- What human supports exist in your school for teachers?
- What other human supports do you think might be helpful to introduce in your school?
- Are your assistant and substitute teachers certified to teach?
- How do parents volunteer at your school?
- How can students play a role in reducing the need for disciplinary activity?

NOTES

1. Sadaka, G. (2022, February 12). *Mental health resources which include professional development* [Post]. LinkedIn. https://www.linkedin.com/in/ghadasadaka/recent-activity/

2. Kamenetz, A. (2022, February 2). More than half the teachers are looking for the exits. *Mindshift.* https://www.kqed.org/mindshift/59018/more-than-half-of-teachers-are-looking-for-the-exits-a-poll-says

3. Sahlberg, P. (2022, June 7). New Education Minister Jason Clare can fix the teacher shortage crisis. *The Conversation.* https://theconversation.com/new-education-minister-jason-clare-can-fix-the-teacher-shortage-crisis-but-not-with-labors-election-plan-184321

4. Carver-Thomas, D., Burns, D., Leung, M., & Ondrasek, N. (2022, January 26). *Teacher shortages during the pandemic: How California districts are responding.* The Learning Policy Institute. https://learningpolicyinstitute.org /sites/default/files/product-files/Teacher_Shortages_During_Pandemic_REPORT.pdf

5. Kelly, J. (2022, March 11). Teachers are not to blame for their own burnout. *School Management Plus.* https://www.schoolmanagementplus.com/heads-governors-school-leadership-governance/teachers-are-not-to-blame-for-their-own-burnout/

6. Kelly, Teachers are not to blame.

Chapter 10

Meaningful Mentorship Support and Performance Appraisal

We began with approximately 20% of the staff demonstrating exceptional levels of performance. With this mentorship program in place, the critical mass of exceptional teachers shifted to 45% over the course of one year.[1]

—Barbara Smith

An apprenticeship culture in a school is often facilitated by deliberate mentorship programs. Typically, seasoned teachers are selected and asked by school leaders to provide support for new teachers to the profession. Effective mentorship programs provide additional preparation time for mentoring activities. How mentorship practices are carried out can vary greatly from school to school.

Concerned about the "steady churn of mandates and administrator turnover," Reeves noted that "strength-based coaching from leadership is increasingly rare in schools."[2] Referring to Rath's research,[3] Reeves added, "employees who are coached on their strengths every day are six times as likely to be engaged in their jobs and more than three times as likely to report having an excellent quality of life in general."[4]

In one restructured elementary school, every teaching staff member was either a mentor or a mentee. Mentors were given their own class for half a day but were free in the other half of the school day to provide support to their mentees. One hour each week, the mentor and the mentee met to co-plan a lesson, and the following day, they co-taught the lesson together in the mentee's classroom. The professional conversations when planning were grounded in the context of their co-teaching experiences in the classrooms. The following was noted by Smith:

Rather than relying on a few demonstrations and professional conversations, schools might consider expanding the coaching role to include regular co-planning followed by co-teaching so that supervisors and mentors can gain a deeper understanding of the classroom context, and therefore, more able to provide rich feedback for teachers, both informally, and formally.[5]

Tables 10.1 and 10.2 illustrate sample schedules for a new middle school math teacher and a mentor math teacher that provide time for preparation and ongoing professional learning. Ample time for growth can happen when the 40-hour work week is broken down with fewer instructional hours than what is typically commonplace in schools.

- 10 hours of instructional classes
- 3.75 to 5 hours per week of wellness breaks
- 2.5 hours of homeroom
- 2.5 hours of lunch
- 2 hours of mentor meetings
- 2 to 3 hours of supervision/support
- 13 to 16 hours of prep/professional growth (PG)

Some mentors can also take part in the performance review process. In this way the support and feedback can be aligned with the mentee teacher's professional expectations. Mentors should provide formative feedback on an ongoing basis, which can also guide mentees when they are encouraged to self-assess their own teaching. In some cases the mentor teacher may conduct formal observations that can be considered as part of an overall teacher appraisal or evaluation.

When mentors take on any feedback or performance review roles, it is important that they take part in rigorous specialized professional learning focused on equipping them with the skills and understandings required to make fair and consistent feedback and assessment to support the improvement of the mentee practice. When mentors observe other's teaching and provide feedback through the lens of rigorous professional standards, this, in turn, can support and enhance the mentor's practice as well.

When less than a handful of administrators take on the task of formal observations, this can often be a dreaded activity, squished into the schedule toward the end of the school year, competing with the ongoing demands of school operations. Quality assessment practices, such as opportunities to view the application of feedback and improvement in follow-up lessons, are rare, as there are not enough bodies to manage the process.

Mentors can provide not only the informal feedback weekly throughout the school year, but they can build in professional conversations customized

Table 10.1: Sample New Middle School Math Teacher

	Monday	Tuesday	Wednesday	Thursday	Friday
8:00 a.m.	Grade 7 Homeroom				
8:30 a.m.	Prep/PG	Prep/PG	Prep/PG	Prep/PG	Prep/PG
9:30 a.m.	Prep/PG	Prep/PG	Grade 8 Team Planning with Math Mentor	Prep/PG	Prep/PG
10:30 p.m.	Wellness Break	Wellness Break	Wellness Break	Wellness Break	Wellness Break
11:30 a.m.	Lunch				
12:15 p.m.	Prep/PG	Prep/PG	Prep/PG	Grade 7 Team Planning with Math Mentor	Prep/PG
1:00 p.m.	Grade 8 Math	Grade 8 Math	Grade 8 Math	Grade 8 Team Teaching with Math Mentor	Grade 8 Math
2:00 p.m.	Grade 7 Math	Grade 7 Math	Grade 7 Math	Grade 7 Math	Grade 7 Team Teaching with Math Mentor
3:00 p.m.	Supervision/Support	Prep/PG	Supervision/Support	Prep/PG	Supervision/Support

Table 10.2: Sample Middle School Mentor Math Teacher

	Monday	Tuesday	Wednesday	Thursday	Friday
8:00 a.m.					
8:30 a.m.	Grade 6 Math	Grade 6 Math	Grade 6 Math	Grade 6 Math	Grade 6 Math
9:30 a.m.	Prep/PG	Prep/PG	Grade 8 Math Team Planning	Prep/PG	Grade 4 Math Team Teaching
10:30 p.m.	Prep/PG	Prep/PG	Grade 3 Math Team Teaching	Grade 4 Math Team Planning	Prep/PG
11:30 a.m.			Lunch		
12:15 p.m.	Grade 5 Math Team Planning	Grade 3 Math Team Planning	Prep/PG	Grade 7 Math Team Planning	Prep/PG
1:00 p.m.	Wellness Break	Wellness Break	Wellness Break	Grade 8 Math Team Teaching	Wellness Break
2:00 p.m.	Prep/PG	Grade 5 Math Team Teaching	Prep/PG	Wellness Break	Grade 7 Math Team Teaching
3:00 p.m.	Supervision/Support	Prep/PG	Supervision/Support	Prep/PG	Prep/PG

for their mentees specifically pertaining to their classroom context. When administrators work in dense teacher-to-supervisor situations, where one supervisor has more than eight direct reports, the quality of staff appraisals and the professional support can be limited.

When the school leader takes on the responsibility of observing and appraising too many staff members, it is likely the evaluations will be so general in nature that they may not lead to professional growth. Often, there is the lack of connection to specific expectations and customized professional learning, and the quality of many appraisals can lack substance or any recommendations for change.

Upon review of school records, it is commonplace for teacher evaluations to house glowing reports in documents framed by general categories. Without the time to coordinate rigorous performance reviews in concert with meaningful professional growth experiences, many school leaders simply go through the motion of getting it done. Referring generally to concerns about many appraisal processes for teachers, Reeves claimed,

> The feedback is inconsistent and unfair. It is inaccurate . . . It is wantonly unspecific, leaving the person being evaluated without a clue as to how to improve in the essentials of instruction, assessment, curriculum and classroom management. It is generally given too late to be of any use. We can and must do better in supporting and developing educators.[6]

To address the limitations of the time and capacity of school leaders to appraise all employees, it makes sense to broaden the leadership opportunities for teachers as mentors who are equipped to provide quality feedback and support for improvement as well as legitimate appreciation of teaching strengths.

Teaching is both an art and science; the appraisal of one's body of work, therefore, should not be captured on a single-page dashboard listing the days absent, a completion of observations, and student test scores. Quality appraisals should require teachers to share their experiences in the form of a professional portfolio that weaves together one's goals with qualifications, workshops, student work samples, parent communications, responses to professional readings, self-reflections, and perhaps action research revealing trials of varied teaching and learning practices.

A small leadership team cannot manage to conduct quality observations and appraisals, let alone muster sincere attention to dozens of professional portfolios. With overloaded proportions of direct reports, many school administrators can go through the motions of staff assessment—not a productive use of their time.

With a larger team of teacher-leaders, teachers can respect and appreciate the feedback and support, especially if it is coming from mentors who are more closely tuned into what's happening in the classroom on a regular basis. Mentors can also be more attentive when discussing and sharing evidence that might be included in their mentee's professional portfolios.

Schools can reconsider how to shift staffing roles to accommodate for better teacher supports and recognition. The flattening of leadership structures in schools can work in scenarios where teacher-leaders can teach half days and use the other half of the school day to plan for classes, plan professional activities for the staff, and support other teachers in regular co-planning and co-teaching experiences.

Teachers who may not want to take on principal or vice principal roles might be interested in middle-management, mentor-type responsibilities, especially if they do not have to give up their classrooms completely, with compensations such as 3 hours of daily preparation. Schools crawling with teacher-leaders would not be a bad thing; in fact, such practices could significantly shift school cultures in the direction of cultivating a more empowered and committed teaching force.

Finally, the cost of development and restructuring can be far less expensive than the cost associated with teacher turnovers. While a staff can benefit from fresh ideas with new staff, it makes sense to keep such numbers manageable to under 10% or 15%. Patrick and Carver Thomas noted the following:

> Urban districts can, on average, spend more than $20,000 on each new hire, including school and district expenses related to separation, recruitment, hiring, and training . . . Addressing teacher turnover is key to stemming shortages nationwide, as about 90% of the annual demand for teachers_is created when teachers leave the profession, with two thirds of teachers leaving for reasons other than retirement.[7]

Teacher turnover is now much more than the situation where teachers transfer in and out of schools. Today schools share a deeper responsibility—that is, to do what they can—to keep teachers from transferring out of the profession altogether. More mentorship supports and quality systems of feedback and appraisals can be significant factors in making teaching a more fulfilling career.

CHALLENGE CHAT

- Describe how mentorship programs do or could support teachers in your school.

- Do you think having mentors who teach part-time and mentor part-time would work in your school?
- Who is responsible for teacher evaluation?
- Do your teachers use professional portfolios, and if so, who do they share them with?
- Why do think it is okay to have some teacher turnover in a school?

NOTES

1. Smith, B. J. (2021). *How much does a great school cost? School economies and values.* Lanham, Maryland: Rowman & Littlefield.

2. Reeves, D. B. (2018, May 1). *Seven keys to restoring the teacher pipeline.* ASCD. https://www.ascd.org/el/articles/seven-keys-to-restoring-the-teacher-pipeline

3. Rath, T. (2007). *Strengthfinder 2.0.* New York: Gallup Press.

4. Reeves, *Seven keys to restoring the teacher pipeline.*

5. Smith, B. (2023). *Assessment tools and systems: Meaningful feedback approaches to promote critical and creative thinking.* Lanham, Maryland: Rowman & Littlefield.

6. Reeves, *Seven keys to restoring the teacher pipeline.*

7. Patrick, S. K., & Carver-Thomas, D. (2022, April 14). *Teacher salaries: A key factor in recruitment and retention.* The Learning Policy Institute. https://learningpolicyinstitute.org/blog/teacher-salaries-key-factor-recruitment-and-retention

Chapter 11

Family Communication and Interaction

I remember working together as a family and being relieved that there was no intense pressure for Erin to complete the project on her own or pressure to hide that parents had helped. Instead, it felt fun and exciting to be a sanctioned cocreator. I remember taking pictures for Erin's genealogy tree. She decided to create her tree with her at the top and the generations below her, holding her up.[1]

—Susana Williams Calley

Parents can play a constructive or destructive role in the culture of a school. In the case of Susana, her role as a cocreator clearly contributed to a positive school climate. Some parents, however, can be the source of a teacher's frustration. Teachers expect administrators to protect them from parents who challenge their expertise in cruel and disrespectful ways. Many teachers leaving the profession may miss their students, but many will not miss the helicopter parents who made them the brunt of social media slander.

Schools can address the issue of parental pressure by looking for proactive ways to include and involve families and, in doing so, clarifying the boundaries of school and parent responsibilities. The family project that Susana was referencing was an initiative developed to support and celebrate parents and students working together on social studies or science-related inquiry. Rather than build in scattered responses to homework throughout the school year, parents were invited to become colearners and cocreators with their children on one project per term. Susana was referring to her work with her daughter on their family tree.

In some cases, families brought in real trees with ancestors featured as ornaments. Other family research was laid on a series of logs. The younger students and families (K to grade two) worked on separate projects, such as making and writing community postcards. In another term the older students created their own planets that featured details of physical geography (e.g., rivers, lakes, oceans, and topographic details of land masses), history (e.g., governmental systems), and space science (e.g., placement in the universe relative to the planets in the solar system). The younger students also created a 51st state.

The family projects were an invitation to celebrate imagination and learning together at home. The projects also created a learning avenue and opportunity for families to be part, not simply observers, of the learning in this Leo da Vinci–inspired school in Virginia. The family projects were presented in the evening, where close to 95% of the families and students attended.

Students took one hour to present at their booth, while the parents had a chance to view the other creations; then the parents had their chance to present at the booth. Rather than the staff doing the work of helping each student put together a conventional science fair, they were able to observe how students and families applied learning at home. The interactions in school do not always have to be one-way communications. The family projects gave the parents permission to be colearners and cocreators with their children.

Parents can play a supportive role in a child's education, but it's difficult when many often feel as though they are dancing in the dark. Not only can the curriculum be a not-so-enchanted forest for teachers, with so much jargon and verbiage, it can seem like a worm hole for parents desperate to grab hold of the edges to try and make sense of it. The lack of clarity within the overengineered crafting of schooled curriculum can make it difficult for parents to help their children.

In some cases, parents succumb to the role of helpless bystanders, unable to keep their kids out of harm's way. In other cases, parents are pleased with a system that punts out their children at or near the top of the class rankings. The parents with children in the middle of the pack, however, wind up subsidizing the tutoring industry, hoping that teachers working the night shift can help move their children up the ladder of class rankings.

Parents who hover over their children are often referred to as *helicopter parents*. Such a term seemed to arise at the same time as the introduction of standardized testing that cannibalized most curriculum that emphasized deep thinking and promoted student engagement. Overinvested parents can often use social media to spread discontent about schools and teachers. While more appropriate channels exist for addressing concerns, it can be difficult for schools and families to work as partners when parents participate in such conversations.

Working parents do not have time to fill in the engagement gaps or study to become curriculum designers of project-based learning of the higher-order kind. Frustrated by observing the collateral damage of lost engagement, many high school parents turn to adding more drudgery to their child's plate by enrolling them in more practice preparation programs in hopes that they can discover the magic of trickery within multiple-choice test questions.

All parents want their children to succeed in school, and when some experience firsthand unhappy kids, they worry and often resort to a host of responses. Some may project their frustration at the teachers and the school, but often the shouting matches at kitchen tables are hidden from the educators' view. The ranking of students does not help all students learn, nor does it contribute to a healthy and industrious society.

Meaningful communication between parents, students, and teachers must be more than a box checked on two or more occasions of planned parent-teacher conferences. Such experiences are often dreaded by teachers who need to inform the parents that some children are not meeting expectations as well as others in the class. While teachers may feel relieved that such sessions are limited to three to five minutes, such token communication only escalates the problem with these parents and can fuel a subculture of social media platforms populated by disgruntled parents.

In the first year of operation at the Jalen Rose Leadership Academy in Detroit, Michigan, every parent had a 20-minute opportunity to speak, goal set, and plan with their child's homeroom teacher on the weekend, when families were not working. Teachers were given the Friday off to compensate for this time.

The homeroom teacher met with each of the parents (20 students in each class), and then parents had an opportunity to meet for 10 minutes with specialist teachers. The homeroom teacher had communicated in advance with all the other teachers so the conversation could center around learning skills. All students were encouraged to attend and be part of these conversations. Saturday was a day that worked in this community, but it is important to make sure any day chosen must be culturally sensitive and responsive, respecting the community.

Kevin Bartlett, founding director of the Common Ground Collaborative, suggests that "curated learning conversations"[2] can be used when the teacher and the student discuss their work during parent-teacher-student conferences. Different from student-led conferences, the curated learning can be observed by the parents, who are invited to contribute to the learning review and goal-setting activity by offering ideas about how they can support student learning at home. "In this way parents have a window into how the teacher interacts with their child, having access to these fishbowl-like discussion, leaving no mystery about next steps."[3]

Students who take part in such conversations have already discussed and self-assessed (not rehearsed) their work prior to these more public conversations. The conventional parent-student conference, where the teacher describes how the student is doing in a small fraction of time, leaves out the key learner. Letting the parent know what the student needs to do to improve when the student is not present creates a disconnect. Having all the players in the room at the same time, hearing the same message, can be much more effective.

Each school calendar highlights precious times for parents to interact and contribute to the school community. Parents are often welcomed in volunteer roles, particularly when organizing community events such as school fairs, welcome-back barbeques, and fund-raising. They can play a key role in spirit building at a school. The teachers can only blow up so many balloons and serve up so many hotdogs. Having a supportive parent community can collectively contribute a host of talents to school wellness and a positive school climate.

Many schools organize assemblies for their students and often for parents at the same time. Students can share their poems, speeches, and skits and announce various student council events. Some schools have assemblies daily, once a week, once a month, or once a term. When parents are part of the audience, there can be more stress to try and make the student presentations spotless, so there can be an argument for parents attending some but not all assemblies, making room for more informal events.

Making mistakes is a key part of learning, and while students and teachers can see the assembly as a forum for learning, it might not be good for students if parents could compare and judge student work in regular public forums. The time taken to prepare assemblies can be disruptive at times, so the frequency of assemblies needs to be part of staff discussions. Once a month can provide a powerful authentic medium for sharing, but weekly or daily may be considered a tad overengineered.

Just as working parents have difficulty being at everything after hours, so too can an abundance of social activities tax the energy of teachers. Families can be encouraged to take part in learning activities organized by the school (i.e., family math). Once a term, optional parent education activities can be coordinated in many schools to give parents an opportunity to inquire about various school initiatives. These Leo Talk events can be similar to TED Talks but with more interaction. In Virginia the families also coordinated a road trip to the NASA Family Space Camp in Huntsville, Alabama.

The number of ways families can be included as part of a school community can vary. The answer to parents who wish to interfere in the workings of the school is not to ban them from entering the school. Just as teachers tend to feel more at home in a school when they are accepted, most parents do too. Schools can work at cultivating mindsets that lead to a building of positive memories rather than filling in a calendar with a volume of obligations.

The value of welcoming communication between the school and home can be priceless.

Responses to annual parent, student, and staff surveys can also provide feedback that can shape meaningful parent activity and doable frequencies. Planning, as well, can take place over two-year blocks so that there is room for new families to the school to share new ideas that can keep the community always eager to ask, "What's next?"

CHALLENGE CHAT

- In what ways is time for feedback and reporting used wisely—or not—in your school?
- How much time do you think is enough to co-plan with parents the next steps to support learning or to delve deeply into a student-led conference about their learning?
- What are your thoughts about curated conversations?
- If conferencing was scheduled for a nonschool day so more families could come, would it be okay if the school gave teachers a day off during the week to compensate for the extra day?
- What would be the barriers to increasing time for reporting on student progress?
- How many social activities with the community are doable for teachers to attend? What factors did you consider when choosing the number for how many?
- How many formal assemblies with parents in the audience do you think should happen during the school year?
- What kinds of parent-education programs are available for your parents?

NOTES

1. S. Williams Caliey, Facebook message personal communication, May 25, 2022.
2. Bartlett, K., founding director of the Common Ground Collaborative. In B. J. Smith's *Assessment tools and systems*.
3. Bartlett, In B. J. Smith's *Assessment tools and systems*.

Chapter 12

Ample Access to Resources

> *We have a copy machine for teacher use, but it may be haunted . . . I have used it exactly 12 times this year (I usually make all of my copies during the weekend), and the copier has broken down or become massively jammed exactly 11 times.*[1]
>
> —Anonymous teacher blogger

While the photocopier may not be the most impactful resource, it can nonetheless harbor deep frustrations when teachers depend on it in a timely manner. Human resources, however, in terms of classroom and professional supports, tend to be what teachers want the most. While chapter 9 focused on supports of the people kind, chapter 12 will address impactful resources of the nonhuman variety.

The resources available for teachers tend to be either prescriptive or material written at a high-level view of curriculum. The recipe-type materials are often prepared in textbooks or leveled readers, whereas the higher-level curriculum resources require a significant amount of time to examine current practice through such a lens and then more time to redesign programs.

Some prescriptive resources integrate peer-reviewed research, while others, not so much.

When a teacher needs more resources, it usually means that a school system has not allocated for a fair acquisition and distribution of materials. However, it could mean that school administrators no longer support a particular approach or they have not committed time, energy, and educational support to help teachers use resources that are intended to change practice.

There are many storerooms in schools that are jam-packed with textbook series designed by former test makers. The assumption held by schools and districts is that such resources would not be as effective as the new texts created by the most current holder of the standardized test design. No wonder education is a billion-dollar industry.

Resources may be vetted by academic leaders, or teachers may be interested in piloting various materials. Resources should support a curriculum that the teachers and school leaders develop together. A resource—program or textbook—by itself should not be considered *the* curriculum. The most engaging materials will have solid connections to the school mission and learning expectations and can often influence feedback and assessment practices.

Harvard's Project Zero (PZ) has been the destination for thousands of educators for many decades. Such professional experiences highlight how teaching for understanding requires that students and teachers be engaged with the learning in ways that promote deeper learning. Since 1967 PZ has made a significant impact on progressive schools. PZ is committed to the following:

> Melding theory and practice, we continue to work toward more enlightened educational processes and systems that support learners, individually and in community, to thrive in, reflect on, contribute to, and change the world in which they will live.[2]

PZ workshops can orient educators to over 60 thinking routines including *visible thinking*. According to education coach Jorge Valenzuela, the following is true:

> Many teachers are looking to adapt research-based methods to help students think about content in meaningful ways by making connections to previous learning, asking relevant questions, displaying understanding through learning artifacts, and identifying their challenges with the material.[3]

Academic leaders in schools should be well acquainted with Harvard Project Zero, as well as Costa and Kallick's highly acclaimed Habits of Mind resources.[4] Linda Nathan, director at Perrone Sizer Institute for Creative Leadership, shared the following:

> At the Boston Arts Academy we want graduates to possess the habit of invention, the habit of refining work, the habit of making connections and last, but certainly not least, the habit of ownership. The work must matter to the maker, and the maker must take responsibility for the making of the work.[5]

Each school or district that applies the habits of mind contributes to the growing body of knowledge of teaching and learning. Two districts in New York City were supported by a three-year grant to build teacher and administrative capacity for supporting a challenging and rigorous curriculum design that addressed culturally responsive sustained education, social and emotional well-being, habits of mind, and the 16 dispositions of effective thinkers.

Forty-five schools in each district were informed by the Learner Centered Initiatives (LCI) and the Institute for Habits of Mind (IHOM).

Kallick shared the following findings: What we learned so far:

- Students are feeling less able to manage themselves in a social and challenging school environment by becoming attentive to their social and emotional needs as well as using the habits of mind to cultivate their capacities as thinkers. Students made tremendous gains when teachers encouraged them to voice their social and emotional needs and use the habits of mind to become aware of their capacities as thinkers and learners.
- Administrators and teachers were able to encourage practices such as learning walks and PLC (professional learning communities) groups to provide opportunities for follow through from training sessions.[6]

There are so many consultants vying for the school administrator's attention. Many have decades of classroom and research experience; others do not. Some will have thick documents filled with data wall charts claiming a paint-by-numbers approach to learning as *the* answer.

The experts who provide supports that adapt to each school context should receive more serious consideration. For instance, Bena Kallick acknowledged that "LCI did not direct us to replicate projects and information exactly the way it was presented to us."[7] She added, "The LCI program inspired us to apply our learning thoughtfully to meet the unique needs of students and teachers in our school," and noted that "it enabled PS228 teachers and students to experience the joy of learning through discovery, collaboration and taking ownership of our learning."[8]

Advisors who support an open-ended and rigorous process for change are far more effective at bringing about positive change and informed practices than those who claim to have all the answers. Kallick shared concrete descriptions of quality professional learning in these New York school districts:

> The professional learning experience motivated us to try out best teaching practices, sparking excitement, curiosity, and a collaborative spirit among members of our teacher team. It fueled the passion within us to support and engage all learners in our school community, which includes a high percentage of English Language Learners and students with IEPs. . . . The program enhanced professional collaboration. Together, we planned authentic, project-based learning for first graders. We reworked learning targets, questions & prompts, strategies, supportive templates, rubrics, and charts. Our team shared with colleagues during school-wide professional learning sessions. We refined teaching and

learning by reflecting on student work, analyzing video clips and planning next steps for ourselves and our students.[9]

Kallick's influence reaches beyond the state or national (US) level. In Brazil at the Escola Concept international bilingual school, each division from the lower school to the high school focused on using habits of minds to support developing explorers (early years), researchers in the lower school, designers in the middle school, and innovative global citizens in the high school. She shared,

> In each of the four divisions, learners apply habits of mind to their daily actions, use the language of thinking to communicate, and understand how to apply the elements of design thinking to problem solve and innovate. As protagonists of this experience, learners use the framework of habits of mind to self-assess their development. One of the main goals is to ensure learners are developing social-emotional skills and dispositions. The evidence that this is being achieved comes through their capacity of identifying, repeating, and embodying the behaviors that support the habits of mind they are enculturating to continuously grow their thinking and learning.[10]

Schools that deliberately seek out ways to design the teaching around the idea of making a positive impact in the world represent exemplars that dare to move from good to great. At Escola Concept, "the academic program is designed to nurture the dispositions of lifelong learners who collaborate to cocreate, embrace an entrepreneurial mindset, understand the meaning of living sustainably, and are globally and digitally fluent."[11] Kallick describes how each part of the school builds on each other.

> As explorers [early years], learners are inspired to practice investigative thinking and tinkering through the use of design thinking processes, which will promote curiosity and inquiry. Responding with wonderment and awe, creating, imagining, and innovating, and gathering data through all senses are the three habits of mind that are thoughtfully enforced with this age group.[12]

What researchers do in the lower school builds on the early years foundation of a "Reggio-inspired approach, the proximity to nature, and the use of deconstructed materials and repurposed objects, [and] learners are provoked to grow their thinking and self-confidence, while developing identity and belonging."[13] Kallick notes that the lower school researchers

> apply the habits of mind of remaining open to continuous learning and thinking flexibly to the design thinking process. Phenomenon-based learning supports the journey in which the generation of hypotheses and the creation of multiple

iterations along the cycle are part of the path to get to the prototype and final product.[14]

It is evident that student engagement fills the classrooms in such environments. Such inquiry-based experiences lead smoothly to middle school *designers*, inspired by Stanford's school, where "learners are active participants in exploring essential questions that are connected to the UN global goals."[15] Kallick shared that here, students "work collaboratively in groups to design solutions to the questions they are exploring," noting,

> These questions connect to the content that is being taught in their classes. They empathize with the problem, define it, perform research, ideate, prototype, and test their solutions which can be a service or a product . . . they learn to take responsible risks, while understanding that failure is an integral part of the process. Festivals and presentations are scheduled where they showcase their work and share lessons learned.[16]

Finally, the high school's "innovative global citizens" generate a culminating project "of impact" that focuses on human-centered design. These students explore the habits of mind that include "remaining open to continuous learning" and "communicating with clarity and precision," while seeking answers to questions such as the following:

- What is design thinking?
- Who am I, and why is self-awareness important in design?
- What are strategies I can use to explore to understand problems and needs that people face; create innovative products and experiences that benefit others; and test my assumptions and verify that my ideas are benefiting others?
- How might I practice being a responsible and ethical designer who is aware of the power and impact of my designs?[17]

The most effective experts and supports for schools combine both detailing with adaptation. The people, the commitment to change, and access to stimulating resources can lay the groundwork for promoting innovative and engaging teaching and learning practices. Viewing a school through the lens of the habits of mind is a powerful way forward.

Rather than featuring subjects and letter grades, the following sample in Table 12.1 illustrates how the emphasis on building habits fits the more current mode of teaching and learning.

How students engage in different subjects may amass varied quantities of evidence. Viewing the student's ongoing learning story through such an

Table 12.1: Sample Habits-of-Mind-Inspired Report Card or Learning Portfolio Assessment

Learning Habits A = ample evidence; B = some evidence; NY = not yet	Language Arts	Math	Science	Social Studies	Physical Education	Arts/ Music; Visual Arts; Drama	Social and Emotional Development (health, character ed., leadership, etc.)
Creating, imagining, innovating							
Listening with understanding and empathy							
Questioning and posing problems							
Gathering data through all senses							
Applying past knowledge to new situations							
Persisting							
Thinking flexibly							
Thinking about your thinking							
Finding humor							
Thinking and communicating with clarity and precision							
Taking responsible risks							
Striving for accuracy							
Remaining open to continuous learning							
Responding with wonderment and awe							
Managing impulsivity							
Thinking interdependently							

adapted lens as habits of mind can provide much more of a contoured, contextual, and meaningful metric for examining student success.

If schools are committed to quality, then qualitative tools such as portfolios should be a serious consideration moving forward.

Educators committed to improving curriculum prospects may consider the prospect of using quality resources to inform innovations in assessment, including a revision of the traditional report card created for students in the former century. As teachers grapple with resources, they may recommend rethinking the *now* and be hands on with the *next*. Curriculum materials that permit such flexibility are rooted in sound educational research.

It can be difficult for school leaders to decipher which resources have potential impact and which resources do not. The Habits of Mind lens, from which one could examine the depth and breadth of resources, can be instrumental in not only helping to target the use of more effective tools but reduce the significant waste of ad hoc school purchases.

A curriculum leader in a school needs to guide the process of resource selection based on their pedagogic understandings. It is not enough to know how various digital tools work; an academic leader should be able to design the scope and sequences of learning and be adept at developing teacher-leaders to collectively build curriculum maps. Technology teachers can aid curriculum leaders by making digital tools available, but the tools themselves cannot drive a quality curriculum.

Building the technology reserves in a school with the most current updated wires and boxes is a popular strategy employed to "fix" and modernize education. Policies grounded in equity often skip the step of examining effective and meaningful ways technology can be implemented or whether technology should be employed just because it is available. As technology specialist Ben Rimes noted,

> Technology will never afford the same "swiss army knife" like tool that is the human mind, able to adapt to a wide variety of needs, one of which might include the need to turn off the technology for a particular learning experience.[18]

When two students share a single screen, there are more opportunities for deeper learning of the interactive and coconstructive kind. Shared classroom devices during in-person learning sessions can work well, so long as the curriculum and teacher-development programs can illustrate how technology and partner activity can be effective. Students should have a mix of opportunities to demonstrate what they know—on their own and with others—just as employers do in the world of work.

As much as teachers should not feel as though they are swimming in a sea of unrealistic curriculum expectations, they must not be expected to implement all the resources and gadgets that exist for teachers today. A streamlined curriculum that is doable should not only recommend suitable resources, it will be flexible enough for teachers to recommend new materials or develop their own supports for their classrooms.

Teachers being forced to use resources they may not understand or value contributes to a culture that undermines the professionalism of educators. Blecher noted that the administrator should inform teachers about what new materials are being rolled out. Having a timeline for learning about the new "product" should include time for "trying it out and sharing feedback."[19] She added, "If the product doesn't fit, it should be acceptable not to adopt it."[20] Rarely do resources come with return policies, so it can be expensive to reverse decisions about the implementation of new resources.

Too often, teachers are left to purchase materials for their classroom from their own savings. Security can be an issue when teachers share their personal cell numbers with families. As Blecher noted,

> Teachers will use their personal laptops and cell phones throughout the school day. That means students and parents/guardians have access to personal cell phone numbers. That's a security breech that makes teachers uncomfortable. Want teachers to be accessible? Provide them with job-paid-for mobile phones and laptops.[21]

Blecher added concern over districts that recommend or suggest certain materials or adopt textbooks series but do not provide the funds for their purchase: "It becomes the haves and have nots."[22] This perpetuates inequities when some teachers can afford to buy resources and others cannot.

Some resources should align with the goals of the school, while other materials may be specific to the teacher or subject matter. Schools should have a rationale for short- and long-term material acquisitions that coincide with strategic planning and school improvement. Replicating the patterns of spending in past budgets should not be the reason some resources are funded and others are not. The coordination, management, and budgeting of meaningful resources is a core part of building a satisfied and fulfilled educator community.

CHALLENGE CHAT

- Which kind of teaching materials (prescriptive or more open ended) resonate with you?
- What resources do you wish teachers had in the short or long term?
- What materials that teachers pay for out of pocket should schools pay for?

- Everything can be improved, even a commercial resource. Have you ever revised materials to better meet the needs of your students?
- In a perfect world, every teacher would have a _____, and every student would have a _____. Share and discuss why this would be ideal.

NOTES

1. Anonymous blogger. (2015, February 28). The copy machine deserves a beating. *Wordpress*. https://drpezz.wordpress.com/2013/11/03/the-copy-machine-deserves-a-beating/

2. Harvard Project Zero. (2022). What is PZ? Project Zero. http://www.pz.harvard.edu/who-we-are/about

3. Valenzuela, J. (2022, March 3). Boosting critical thinking across the curriculum. Edutopia. George Lucas Foundation. https://www.edutopia.org/article/boosting-critical-thinking-across-curriculum

4. Costa, A. & Kallick, B. (2022). What are habits of mind? The Institute for Habits of Mind. https://www.habitsofmindinstitute.org/what-are-habits-of-mind/

5. Nathan, L. (2014, July 25). We have allowed the state to declare war on schools and teachers. *Boston Review*. https://bostonreview.net/forum_response/linda-nathan-habits-mind/

6. (B. Kallick, email personal communication, June 27, 2022).

7. Kallick, email personal communication.

8. Kallick, email personal communication.

9. Kallick, email personal communication.

10. Kallick, email personal communication.

11. Kallick, email personal communication.

12. Kallick, email personal communication.

13. Kallick, email personal communication.

14. Kallick, email personal communication.

15. Kallick, email personal communication.

16. Kallick, email personal communication.

17. Kallick, email personal communication.

18. Rimes, B. (2014, December 5). Technology will not revolutionize education. *The Tech Savvy Educator*. https://www.techsavvyed.net/archives/3754

19. H. Blecher, email personal communication, July 17, 2022.

20. Blecher, email personal communication.

21. Blecher, email personal communication.

22. Blecher, email personal communication.

Chapter 13

Stunning and Stimulating Spaces

> *We've made our school purposefully joyful . . . It means having displays, art, and areas that lets children be imaginative in their thoughts and learning . . . When they have a suggestion, we go with it and let them contribute . . . we believe the outdoors is part of our school. Not just the playground, but the walking trails, parks, and forests that surround us Spending hours (not minutes) outside everyday contributes significantly to happiness, learning, and good mental health. We think we got it right when children say they don't want to go home!*[1]
>
> —John Neretlis, head of school, Brick Labs Academy, Toronto

There are spaces that light up the walls and halls of physical school landmarks, and there are school spaces that respect and support the building of inclusive relationships between community members. Both spaces can provide positive cultural settings, the kind that support an inclusive environment where everyone belongs.

Clean and compelling work sites can set an attractive tone in the workplace. Tired buildings with coffee-stained cups, worn-out bulletin boards, and broken tiles send a message that such places are not worthy of supporting teaching and learning. When a renter looks for an apartment, they can be turned off by rug stains and scuff marks on the doors. It is often the neglect of the small repairs or overdue paint work that can shape a perception that care has not been taken to maintain or enhance learning spaces.

Just as Disney transformed the image of a dirty carnival into a clean and polished amusement park, it is time for schools to reshape the look and feel of many industrial models mimicking factories. Student engagement and teacher fulfillment can be enhanced if schools and teaching were viewed and funded as dignified places of work and study.

Browse the web to find innovative school spaces. There are some stunning samples of architecture with curvy walls and outdoor learning spaces, but there should be many more exemplars of stunning spaces for teaching and learning. For instance, can you imagine cafeteria cubbies that replicate the booths in a restaurant, floor tiles that tell the tale of proud school stories, or the solar system painted on ceiling tiles? Schools do not need to be made of concrete, nor do teachers need to see the trails of tired broken bricks, not tended to for years.

Children's hospitals have been highly innovative in their designs. At Sick Kids Hospital in Toronto, they replaced the antiseptic condo entranceway's look and feel with creative, fun, and customized themes without compromising cleanliness. What if each school could be unique and follow the lead of Disney or the Sick Kids Hospital?

At a school in Virginia, local artists donated their time to create murals in the primary wing featuring Jack and the Beanstalk, but the image also integrated key features of the horsing community. The upper-grade mural focused on a yellow brick road highlighting the images of social justice and the school's charter of rights. The staff room was renamed the Inspiration Room, complete with a professional library, photocopying machine, and coffee maker.

It's unfair that some schools can showcase facilities that inspire, while others do not. According to Harris, Kolodner, and Morton, "Many districts with bustling main streets and abundant resources can erect gleaming modern facilities, while districts with boarded-up storefronts and with little property wealth have little to nothing set aside to patch up crumbling infrastructure."[2]

Such claims are further supported in their Hechinger Report, which documents further evidence of school inequalities: "From classrooms with air in Baltimore to deteriorating-facilities in the Mississippi Delta, school infrastructure often follows the pattern of the nation's most entrenched inequalities, intertwining closely with race and wealth."[3]

Dave Steiber noted neglected facilities in many schools contribute to "demoralizing teachers."[4]

> Having to tape down broken asbestos tiles on our floor so the students and staff don't breathe in a carcinogen . . . we also try to ignore that it's only 60 degrees in our classroom in the dead of winter or that it's over 90 degrees in our rooms in the summer. We try to ignore the mold in the ceiling tiles, the windows that don't open, the blinds that broke and have not been repaired, ever, and the floors that haven't been swept because every custodian has quit.[5]

It is much easier to clean and maintain a smaller building than the large superstructures that have become the norm in many US schools. Teachers should not have to teach and students should not have to learn in a warehouse.

Teachers need to work in stimulating environments. It's stimulating when the students you work with not only learn but are enthusiastic about what they are learning. Some teachers may need more resources, while others may need the budget and time to create new learning materials to enhance the learning experience.

The décor in a school can be overdone. Concerned about distraction, Blecher claimed the following:

> The classroom shouldn't be filled with so many store-bought posters and signs that it becomes overstimulating and thus thwarts learning . . . classroom décor shouldn't pit one teacher against another. I worked in one school where we didn't decorate the classroom ahead of time. What was put up on the walls was there to connect to what was being taught at that time. What a difference this made for staff and students.[6]

It's stimulating when colleagues are eager to mentor each other, share resources, take part in or present at conferences, engage in action research, team-teach, and simply have fun with one another. Time for professional growth and time to develop a positive school climate should never be considered extra. Support for the development of collegial relationships helps to keep teachers wanting to return and contribute to the greater good of the school.

CHALLENGE CHAT

- In what ways does your school make it stimulating for professional educators?
- What else could your school do to make teachers, students, and parents feel included?
- What would be the barriers to bringing about a more stimulating school culture?
- Who could support improving a school culture, and what could they actually do to demonstrate that support?

NOTES

1. Neretlis, J. (2022, February). We've made our school purposefully joyful. It means having displays, art, and areas that lets children be imaginative in their [Post]. LinkedIn. https://www.linkedin.com/in/john-neretlis-mba-970385b8/recent-activity/

2. Harris, B., Kolodner, M., & Morton, N. (2020, November 2). Rundown schools forced more students to go remote. *The Hechinger Report*. https://hechingerreport.org/rundown-schools-forced-more-students-to-go-remote

3. Harris, Rundown schools forced more.

4. Stieber, D. (2022, February 14). America's teachers aren't burned out: We are demoralized. *EdSurge*. https://www.edsurge.com/news/2022-02-14-america-s-teachers-aren-t-burned-out-we-are-demoralized

5. Stieber, America's teachers aren't burned out.

6. (H. Blecher, email personal communication, July 17, 2022).

Chapter 14

Teacher Leadership Opportunities

I wasn't sure what I was taking on, but I knew that if I had not taken the role [leadership role], I might not have stayed in education.[1]

—Doctoral student candidate

This quote was shared by Candace McQueen, CEO of the National Institute for Excellence in Teaching (NIET) in the United States. She recounted the teacher-leader journey of one of her peers two decades ago in her doctoral program. In her article, McQueen seemed to yearn for the return of such interest and passion in school leadership:

> She spoke with such authority about how her advancement into a teacher leader role was the difference-maker for why she stayed in the profession and why she would eventually move into a principalship and then to a district leadership role. I vividly remember her passion for creating these formal pathways that support retention and advancement of top teachers.[2]

Beyond the perils of the recent management of COVID-19 safety protocols, what has changed in 20 years? Teachers nowadays do want a say, but the interest in teacher leadership has waned. McQueen claimed that few teachers aspire or envision being a state leader or policymaker, noting that "Chiefs for Change found that only 5% of teachers expressed an interest in being a chief state school officer."[3]

The question remains, Who gets a say? In an inclusive school environment, school systems may say everyone has a say, but this is not how things work in schools. In actuality, teachers had more say decades ago than they have today. As examined in chapter 5, there is a need for teachers to have more autonomy and a sense that their ideas are respected. The teacher-leader roles could give teachers more say in some things, but there is much that is controlled by the central office or government in education.

In 1997 Zinn researched the supports in place for the development of teacher-leadership roles in schools. She suggested that the "overall structure of schools impedes leadership, as it reinforces teachers' isolation."[4] Zinn concluded that classroom responsibilities limited "available time for leadership endeavors," acknowledging that her study participants agreed that "time looms as the greatest barrier to teacher leadership."[5]

Even when additional time is provided for teacher-leaders in schools, there is a risk that other teachers can be jealous of time freed up for the additional responsibility. Zinn interviewed Title I teacher-leader Mary Elle, who shared her concern about such cultural collateral damage: "Resentment would come around the fact that my job, in itself, provides more flexibility than most jobs here in the building. And they don't like it, because they don't have that."[6]

McQueen shared her personal position on teacher-leadership:

> When I look back on the last twenty years of my career, I can see the influence of teacher leaders because they have directly helped me to teach more effectively and informed my role as a policymaker. But, maybe more importantly, I have hired, promoted, elevated, and sought the advice of teacher leaders to ensure our profession learns and grows from those who know it best. I am confident that if we create more teacher leadership pathways, every part of our education system . . . will be better off.[7]

Apart from preparing future school leaders, there are significant reasons why schools need to establish teacher-leadership pipelines—notably, to increase student achievement and teacher retention. The New Teacher Center (NTC) reported that "students in schools with the highest levels of reported instructional and teacher leadership performed up to 10 percentage points higher in math and English language arts, compared to schools with the lowest levels."[8]

The research of the National Institute for Excellence in Teaching (NIET) of over 12,000 teachers across 10 states confirmed that teacher retention rates were 14% higher in schools with teacher-leaders.[9] According to Alan Todd, "Plain and simple, leadership development programs are good for business. According to Gallup, companies prioritizing leadership development can expect employee engagement rates to double and earnings-per share to increase 147%."[10]

School leaders do not benefit from operating in isolation. The more they can surround themselves with talent who can support teachers, the more schools can be ideal places for teaching and learning. Many educational experts agree that education needs to change; they just are unsure which of the buffet of change options should happen and which ones should be implemented first.

Flattening the leadership stream to invite more teachers into leadership roles can help decipher and determine school priorities.

Concerned about the aftermath of "two and a half decades of toxic policies" that punish and reward school systems "based largely on terminating or moving principals," Doug Reeves claimed that such practices have "led to teachers being at sea amid a squall of inconsistent initiatives and demands."[11] He went on to add, "The resulting cynicism prevents the effective implementation of even the most promising ideas."[12] To make matters worse, Renee Owen from Southern Oregon University explains,

> Administrator licensure programs primarily train new leaders to comply with current laws and systems; they aren't training administrators to be revolutionary! So not only are our public school systems not designed for second-order change—which requires changes in beliefs and behaviors—but our leaders are not trained for transformative change.[13]

How can existing school leaders support their teachers if they are not equipped to implement disruptive change?

In many ways it seems as if the "higher ups" really do not want to invite significant change—or perhaps only the appearance of it through the transmission of volumes and volumes of documents labeled as initiatives. But are the initiatives sustainable, or are they worthy of the effort to implement them?

French and Prendergast interviewed Anna for their article, "Systems and Structures for Keeping Your Best Teachers," who claimed that teachers need to be part of an initiative inventory. Anna shared how the process worked for her:

> The leaders had already culled down loads of things into buckets, or *like categories*, and we broke into teams to rank things by how important they were to student learning, or to doing our job, for example. My principal is [currently] looking at all our ideas and coming back with a plan of how we'll dig deeper on just some tools and make others optional to use.[14]

They noted the following:

> Taking time to sort through the clutter helps everyone prioritize *and* elevates consistency across classrooms. As important, hearing administrators articulate why resources were selected to support student learning helps teachers understand the maze of options and see the bigger picture.[15]

A different Anna interviewed by Michael Lawrence (for his book that compares Finnish and Australian education) described herself in the past as a "flipping great teacher" for over 30 years, moved by the "joy of engaging students . . . seeing them succeed when they thought they couldn't."[16] Unfortunately, Anna no longer feels the same way. Rather, she confided the following:

> I became broken by the system that was relentless in its need to add to my to-do list with administrative task after administrative task . . . and by parents who were empowered in the system to micromanage every aspect of their child's learning and throw blame at the drop of a hat in a teacher's direction.[17]

Whether Anna was from Australia, the UK, Canada, or the United States, it doesn't matter, as this story is sad but true on many continents.

The lack of coordination of initiatives can be so disruptive that many teachers nod their heads and pretend to accept new policies, but without a voice and pathways to positions of responsibility, they can feel lost and disenfranchised. There is so much talk about inclusion, but rarely are teachers included in the designing of their own school curriculum. When the standards became the curriculum, many teachers lost their passion and desire for improving the profession. How, then, can the culture of "just tell me what to do" transform to "look how we can build better schools!"?

The joy of helping others as a teacher-leader may not be enough to change the course of teacher shortages happening now or pending in Western civilizations, but bringing more teacher voices into the fold to not own the initiatives of others but develop their own initiatives can be at the core of changing a culture knee-deep in compliance and all things bureaucratic.

Disruptive change is rarely expected from district-level supervisors or higher ups, but it is exactly what is required to make teaching more fulfilling and learning more engaging. The gatekeepers may frown upon systematic restructuring, but that doesn't mean that teachers should be apathetic and give up on schools. Teacher education institutions can develop lab schools to demonstrate how peer-reviewed research can inform practice and how practice can inform theory. Educational experts should lead educational change, not follow a faulty system.

Teachers and bold school leaders can make room for more leadership roles and make sound arguments for adding more bodies in schools that can free up teacher-leaders to support teachers. There are so many ways to be a school leader beyond publishing in peer-reviewed journals. Teachers can present at conferences as well as host and organize them. Such opportunities provide excellent growth experiences.

An inspired culture can be built with people whose imaginations, creativity, and capacity to innovate are not constrained. How often is a new school opened that replicated another school? Too often. For each new school that is approved, there should be hundreds of new offers to meet the varied needs of students, teachers, and communities. More laboratory schools should inform the budgets, curricula, staffing, and physical plants of new schools. Educational innovation needs more spaces to thrive. According to Nordengren (2016),

> We believe a professional culture built around teachers as leaders is optimal for attracting, developing, and retaining the best kindergarten–12 teachers. Leadership is expected from beginning teachers, argues Nathan Bond in the Educational Forum, as novice teachers "are expected to function at the same level as veterans in terms of instruction in the classroom and engagement in the activities in the larger school community."[18]

Teacher-leaders can coordinate action research and books clubs; they do not simply go to conferences but present at them or, better yet, organize them. Teacher-leaders can coordinate social events and school spirit in a valued role as VP of school culture. Teacher-leaders can keep a pulse on school wellness; they can coordinate professional learning activities with other schools. They can share engaging teaching and learning experiences in a TED Talk. They can become Habits of Mind consultants; they can teach continuing education courses. They can write curriculum resources and publish them!

The Alberta Teacher's Federation lists over 35 activities for professional growth, including

- action research,
- book/article study,
- classroom/school visitation and exchanges,
- curriculum development/mapping,
- community service,
- data analysis,
- examining student work,
- education exchange,
- hosting a student teacher,
- integrated curriculum planning,
- lesson study,
- online PD programming,
- networks,
- peer coaching/mentorship,
- taking post-secondary courses,
- professional organizations,
- professional portfolios,
- school improvement teams,
- school based workshops,

- retreats, [and]
- videoconferencing.[19]

They can do much more than gaze at data walls.

Sharing can take the form of making connections at a conference as delegates or presenters, engaging with others in webinars, or working on cross-school action research projects. For instance, the Toronto Boys' School Coalition formed a group that examined teaching and learning conditions that might be specific for boys.

In many charter schools in the United States, there is a growing tendency to hire school leaders with little or no classroom experience. Such a practice ignores the notion that each leader in the chain of command understands the role of their direct reports. How can someone in a lead role evaluate the academic leader—for instance, in a school—if they have never taught in a classroom? In such cases there is a naïve overreliance on data dashboards, which only provide a glimpse of what's happening in a school.

The politicians that sanction uncertified teachers often support unqualified school leaders. As McQueen claims, "To improve education, we need more educational decision-makers and leaders to have classroom experience."[20] She added, "If we do not create more of these opportunities and encourage educators to step into them, we will lose out on ensuring decisions that affect the classroom are made by those who understand classroom practice."[21]

Certain teachers may be committed to improving different areas of a school, so it is important for school leaders to develop opportunities for shared leadership, honoring the varied voices and initiatives of teacher-leaders. The school leader may determine some key goals for the school but must be careful not to project a vision that all must jump on board or get out the way.

A realistic school leader will invite input from teachers. Innovators will know that some teachers will be inspired by change right away, while others may need more convincing that students will truly benefit from new ways of doing things in the school.

CHALLENGE CHAT

1. What kinds of teacher-leadership positions could benefit your school?
2. In what way can you develop as a prospect for a teacher-leader position?
3. Why should teacher-leaders be aware of action research?
4. How long should someone teach in a classroom or school setting before being able to apply for an administrative role?
5. Do you think school leaders should have classroom experience? Discuss.

NOTES

1. Anonymous graduate student. (2020, May 20). In C. McQueen *The one-two punch of teacher-leadership*. National Institute for Excellence in Teaching. https://www.niet.org/newsroom/show/blog/one-two-punch-of-teacher-leadership-candice-mcqueen

2. McQueen, C. (2020, May 20). *The one-two punch of leadership*. NIET (National Institute for Excellence in Teaching). https://www.niet.org/newsroom/show/blog/one-two-punch-of-teacher-leadership-candice-mcqueen

3. McQueen, *The one-two punch of leadership*.

4. Zinn, L. F. (1997). *Supports and barriers to teacher leadership: Reports of teacher leaders*. AERA. https://lsc-net.terc.edu/do/paper/8120/show/page-3/use_set-ldrshp.html

5. Zinn, *Supports and barriers*.

6. Zinn, *Supports and barriers*.

7. McQueen, *The one-two punch of leadership*.

8. McQueen, *The one-two punch of leadership*.

9. McQueen, *The one-two punch of leadership*.

10. Todd, A. (2021, September). How to build leadership capabilities that'll keep your employees engaged. *Udemy*. https://blog.udemy.com/leadership-training-topics/

11. Reeves, D. B. (2018, May 1). Seven keys to restoring the teacher pipeline. *ASCD*. https://www.ascd.org/el/articles/seven-keys-to-restoring-the-teacher-pipeline

12. Reeves, Seven keys to restoring.

13. Owen, R. (2022, April 21). Can we make real, transformative change in education? *Greater Good Magazine*. https://greatergood.berkeley.edu/article/item/can_we_make_real_transformative_change_in_education?fbclid=IwAR1hI4vOTrfqDsVnP3DMC1BolGhGa0tozU74HKget_Zho8vnlqkNXDPDxa0

14. French, A., & Prendergast, L. (2022, May 31). Systems and structures for keeping your best teachers. *ASCD*. https://www.ascd.org/blogs/systems-and-structures-for-keeping-your-best-teachers

15. French, Systems and structures.

16. Lawrence, M. (2020). *Testing 3-2-1: What Australian education can learn from Finland?*

17. Lawrence, *What Australian education*, 187.

18. Nordengren, C. (2016). Educators want opportunities for teacher-leadership, too. *ASCD*. https://www.ascd.org/el/articles/new-educators-want-opportunities-for-teacher-leadership-too

19. Alberta Teacher's Federation. (2023). *PD activities for professional growth*. https://www.teachers.ab.ca/For%20Members/ProfessionalGrowth/Section%203/Pages/Professional%20Development%20Activities%20for%20Teachers.aspx

20. McQueen, *The one-two punch of leadership*.

21. McQueen, *The one-two punch of leadership*.

Chapter 15

Health and Safety

> *We can't expect teachers to work 60–70 hours per week or more, but then tell them to self care. Maybe leaving is their self care? Let's focus on taking care of teachers in the 2022–2023 school year!*[1]
>
> —Dr. Brad Johnson

Caring for a school community is everyone's business. Beyond the generous detailing of health-related benefits, schools can be designed to support wellness and safety in proactive ways. Making schedules and expectations manageable would most likely reduce the need for teachers to use their sick days. A culture that is mindful of safety and wellness is one that can contribute greatly to employee satisfaction.

The idea that the health and safety of a school staff can be narrowed to a provision of self-care programs is not enough. Schools must do more than prioritize resiliency as a solution to mental health problems—for teachers and students. When Dr. Tracy Edwards was asked to share her thoughts about a webinar she attended on resilience, she responded: "I don't want to be resilient. I want school systems designed with humans in mind that don't demand my resilience. I want educators to experience community care, support, and compensation."[2]

The teaching profession should not be a career that permeates chronic stress. Dr. Stephanie Ernestus added, "I am, once again, asking people to stop using resilience as an individual trait (instead of a process or outcome). We gotta stop shifting the blame onto individuals for failing in failing systems."[3] On the same Twitter feed, Sabrina Syed noted, "Resilience doesn't mean increased tolerance for abuse."[4] The solution to chronic stress cannot be rooted in self-care.

Chase Mielke's book *The Burnout Cure: Learning to Love Teaching Again* acknowledges that "countless problems within the educational system are leading to teacher burnout and dissatisfaction."[5] He claimed, however, that "to expend the energy necessary to address large-scale issues . . . educators need to have energy in the first place."[6] His work encourages teachers to learn to think positively and differently by focusing on metacognitions and actions to improve well-being.[7]

The fitness memberships, yoga classes, and other well-being-focused activities should be welcomed additions to any profession. Such responses to the current crisis of teacher retention, however, can be short-lived without changes to the system and a recognition that burnout can be a response to chronic stress. The Leichtman Burnout Scale identifies four levels of burnout symptoms:

- Level 1—passionate but overwhelmed
- Level 2—overwhelmed and becoming cynical
- Level 3—cynical and approaching exhaustion
- Level 4—complete exhaustion and breakdown[8]

Burnout in education is a real crisis, and no matter how much we learn how to think positively or avoid complaining for 48 hours, school leaders need to address not simply some systematic changes, as recommended in the previous chapters, but all of them. If health and wellness are truly valued, then the remaking of schools needs to be a priority.

The costs associated with the number of sick days and short- and long-term leaves in response to unrealistic expectations could be better invested in more teachers, reduced class sizes, and increased preparation time. The responsibility is on the school system to provide healthy working conditions. If the number of students is too many, the number of classes in a day is too much, and the amount of preparation is too little, then the health of teachers will suffer.

In concert with a concern for health and wellness is the distress associated with school safety, especially given the pattern in U.S. schools of violence and school shootings. Metal detectors with the presence of armed police may bring a sense of comfort for some staff members, but more legislation to remove access to weapons in communities may be necessary to assure teachers that their safety as well as the safety of their students matters.

It is alarming that two decades after the Columbine High School shooting in 1999, legislation has not made schools safer. Had serious changes been addressed by politicians at that time, perhaps the world would not be so familiar with Sandy Hook, Marjory Stoneman Douglas, or Robb Elementary. When other countries average less than five shootings and the United States has, over the course of nine years (between 2009 and 2018), 288 shootings, there is reason for people to think twice about being an educator in the United States.

School administrators must ensure that proper lockdown drills take place, that exit doors are locked, and that a comprehensive system of tracking visitors and all school community members is in place. The idea of asking teachers to learn how to use a gun to protect themselves and others would be an added expectation that, for many teachers, might be considered a deterrent. Placing more guns in schools may be one reactive solution, but teachers are not police officers, nor are they at war.

The safety of educators is everyone's responsibility; families may have the right to purchase an AK-47, but that might not be much help if they need to do homeschooling. With teachers leaving, it is inevitable that class sizes will continue to increase, putting more teaching in the hands of parents. If society wants more qualified and talented teachers, then something has to give. Teachers should not have to risk their lives each day they enter a classroom.

For schools to be safe places, it is important to consider the roots of violent problems, and many can be traced back to mental health issues emerging from young people not feeling a sense of belonging. It's hard to belong to a community with over 300 people in it. It's hard to belong in a classroom cultivated on a one-size-fits-all model. It's hard to belong when teachers have little time to develop genuine relationships with their students. It's hard to belong when families are disconnected from schools. It's hard to belong when some students and teachers have access to technology and others do not. It's hard to belong when students and teachers are not well enough to be present at school.

CHALLENGE CHAT

- In what ways is your school safe?
- How well do students and teachers feel in your school? How do you know?
- In what ways can your school improve how all community members feel like they belong?

NOTES

1. Johnson, B. [@DrBradJohnson]. (2022, May 29). We can't expect teachers to work 60–70 hours per week or more, but then tell them to self care [Tweet]. Twitter. https://twitter.com/DrBradJohnson/status/1530957357735460866

2. Edwards, T. [@tracyrenee70]. (2022, March 2). Sat through a webinar on teacher resilience & was asked to share my thoughts. My answer: I don't want to [Tweet]. Twitter. https://twitter.com/tracyrenee70/status/1498812420239675392

3. Ernestus, S. [@DrErnestus]. (2021, September 5). I am, once again, asking people to stop using resilience as an individual trait (instead of a process or outcome) [Tweet]. Twitter. https://twitter.com/DrErnestus/status/1434694860783689734

4. Syed, S. [@MDinWaiting]. (2021, September 3). Did it hurt? When you poured out your trauma to get into med school and were praised for being resilient [Tweet]. Twitter. https://twitter.com/MDinWaiting/status/1433955039899369474

5. Mielke, C. (2019). *The burnout cure: Learning to love teaching again.* Alexandria, Virginia: ASCD.

6. Mielke, *The burnout cure*, 8.

7. Mielke, *The burnout cure*, 10.

8. Leichtman, K. (2022, May 26). How burned out are you? A scale for teachers. *Edutopia*. https://www.edutopia.org/article/how-burned-out-are-you-scale-teachers

Conclusion
I Want to Be a Teacher

Disneyland will never be completed, as long as there is imagination left in the world.[1]

—Walt Disney

Much the same as there is room for improvement at Disney, there should be room for the further development of schools. There are no limits when designers use their imagination. *Teacher Shortages and the Challenge of Retention* is not about returning to the past; rather, it's an invitation to join other educators on a road trip of invention, a tour of how teaching experiences can become more engaging via alternative routes for teacher fulfillment.

Road trips can be methodically planned or they can be reckless pursuits. Both can be memorable and filled with lessons learned along the way. While there is no perfect itinerary and no perfect destination, there are viable and inspiring options worthy of consideration.

Teaching should not be a road for those who fear learning from mistakes. Improvement cannot happen without change, and change is rarely void of bumps along the way. As Renee Owen suggests,

> In schools, there is a constant striving for improvement, but improvement—getting better at what we already do within the systems we already have—will never fundamentally change who we are or how we think. Improvement will never erase inequities. We will continue to get the same results unless we are able to see education in a completely new way.[2]

This particular road trip, paved by decades of experiences, is synthesized as an example for readers to consider powerful alternatives to the current, mixed-up, masked state of affairs or dated bucket used to fill a century of compromises. What might a 22nd century look like if we could snap our fingers and make it so, today?

This road trip is not built with red bricks or science fiction; rather, it is one that recognizes how other professions seemingly drive along on paved freeways, while educators seem to exist and tolerate the bumpiness of a gravel road. Why are the legal or medical professions considered more attractive occupations than teaching? Notwithstanding, each job has its issues, but why are there significantly fewer people today committed to becoming teachers?

Teaching should not be perceived as a sacrifice. It should be viewed as a fulfilling, respected, and meaningful profession. The challenge before us is one that requires North American—and other—societies to collectively change their perception about the teaching career. If schools are valued places, then a cultural shift needs to happen. The status of teaching needs to change. The statement "I do not want to be a teacher" needs to be replaced by "I want to be a teacher."

So what actions can stakeholders take to make teaching a more highly respected and admired occupation? Before randomly piling on incentives, it is important to understand the nature of a culture ready—or not—for change.

A matrix with one continuum representing the commitment to change by various stakeholders on the X-axis and the proposed scale of change on the Y-axis can illustrate relative readiness for developing and implementing widescale change in Figure 16.1.

The likelihood of the adoption of change is complex and linked directly to the mindsets of school stakeholders. Figure 16.1 represents a simple model that serves to navigate this examination of what it could take to increase the status of education in a vast majority of Western-influenced countries around the world.

For change initiatives to stick, there needs to be a high level of commitment to change and agency. Educators need to feel their ideas matter. What often happens is that change is supported—or not—one initiative at a time. Even when there seem to be high levels of commitment to that change, it can often flicker out like a sparkler in the night, not because the initial wave of support did not exist but the lack of energy or fuel to fight the collateral impacts of change.

The school is an interdependent system; any change to one aspect of the operation ultimately influences change in other sectors of the organization. It is in the protection of the "other" seemingly sacred practices where adversity and objection to change can harvest a return to a "good enough" way of doing school.

Make no mistake, decision-makers are influenced by many stakeholders. The government officials who determine the curriculum at the national, state, or provincial level play a significant role in shaping the real estate of

Conclusion

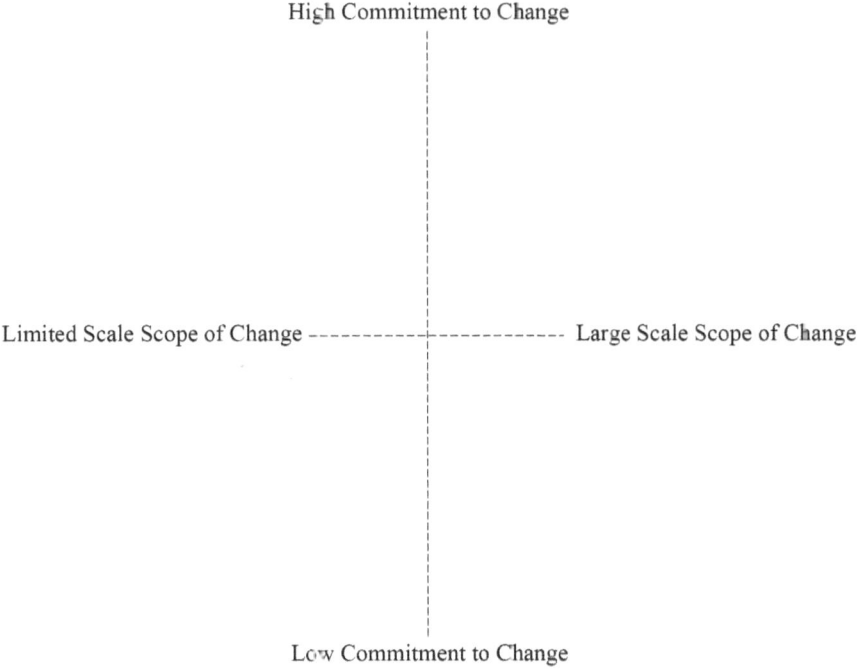

Figure 16.1. Emerging Matrix of School Change Adoption

education. They often need to respond to political directives that may or may not be grounded in current research. In a more direct way, school trustees, who hold the balance of power in terms of funding allocations, can also be influenced by the will to stay elected. Even though trustees are not responsible for the operations in a school or school district, they do make key decisions about school budgets and leadership.

There are layers of hierarchies in schools that are responsible for various branches of education. Apart from national, state, or provincial mandates, in public school systems, the directors of education along with a core of superintendents have enormous potential to influence change. Depending on the school system, there are principals and teachers who can exhibit significant influence on change. Students and teachers, who are closest to the learning context, should have a seat at the table of school change.

Everyone has a role to play in this shift—current decision-makers in schools and particularly parents, trustees, and students. It will take a courageous critical mass to bring about major changes in mindsets before any new systems can emerge from what could be the rubble left behind. It's not enough to write books to teachers and school leaders about change; everyone needs to play a role in supporting a transformation of all kinds of education: public, independent, charter, international, teacher education, what the new tech world of education can offer.

Peeling back the layers of what's not fulfilling and replacing schools with what is appealing is a start. There needs to be more changing forces, not folks willing to settle, because learning is important. To make way for change, society will need to accept a disruption, the kind that detours the current conditions for teaching.

What if the following were true?

- Teachers had salaries comparable to other professions.
- Teachers had fewer than 20 students in their classes.
- Teachers had enough time to polish, prepare, and reflect.
- School schedules provided ample time for most students to master learning.
- Teachers took part in meaningful, ongoing professional learning.
- Teachers had fewer expectations to teach.
- School leaders trusted their teachers' capacities to assess students.
- School leaders respected and recognized teacher insight, action, and creativity.
- Teachers had ample classroom supports.
- There were more mentors available to support new teachers.
- Performance appraisals were connected to professional learning.
- There was ample time for teachers to interact with families.
- Teachers had access to ample resources.
- The workplace setting was renovated and inspiring.
- There were ample opportunities for upward mobility.
- Supervisors had fewer direct reports and more time to provide individual support.
- Health and wellness of community members was paramount.
- More teachers felt safe in their classrooms.

How daunting is such a list of expectations without any give in the system? Educators know these are best practices but recognize they can be pipe dreams for all teachers to experience. Doing any of these recommendations in isolation of a systematic strategic plan would not be as beneficial as a synthesis of all these conditions that can lead to enhanced staff satisfaction at the same time as encouraging potential talent to say, "I want to be a teacher."

Lists only have potency if teachers have a say in generating the items on the list. After all, they do know the barriers to the profession more than anyone. Shifting working conditions needs to be on the minds of all stakeholders. Like Disney, education should be fluid and open to improvement, as teaching should be ever changing, never completed nor perfected. The more there are decision-makers that plug up innovation by going with the flow, the more schooling will simply accept stagnation.

The Stephen Covey quote, "The key is in not spending time, but in investing it,"[3] represents a key starting point for change. As Professor Walter Smith noted, "No profession in the world has to create the system they work in as they go—except for teachers. We need a system to work in like all other professions."[4] The task of improving teaching conditions should not happen in isolation of making ideal schools. We need to think deeply about the kinds of school experiences that could make teachers feel like a million bucks.

Changing working conditions should not be about negotiating demands; all stakeholders must be willing to do what is needed to make teaching a fulfilling and attractive profession. School leaders must not only understand the options but have the strategic vision to ensure their implementation.

It's time to change the water in the school tank . . . it's cloudy and unhealthy after close to a century of taking in and emitting the same nutrients. The inhabitants, teachers, and students alike need fresher sources of sustenance.

Teachers are leaving the swamp; pinning hopes on replenishing the stock is a naïve solution. If school leaders want to get ahead of the serious problem of teacher retention and attraction to the field, they need to learn how to navigate around the rapids in education and find fresh water for all community members to thrive, not simply survive.

If schools can be redesigned to remove existing barriers, perhaps the path might attract more talent and keep our current assets not simply in place but eager to make the profession a more popular option? The hard work of getting more people to say they want to become a teacher is not going to be easy, and even with good intentions that began yesterday, there needs to be a deeper sense of urgency to move the bigger boulders of sameness in schools *now*!

NOTES

1. Fischer, R. (2004). *The creation of Disneyland*. American Beat. http://www.plosin.com/beatbegins/projects/fischer.html.

2. Owen, R. (2022, April 21). Can we make real, transformative change in education? *Greater Good Magazine*. https://greatergood.berkeley.edu/article/item/can_we_make_real_transformative_change_in_education?fbclid=IwAR1hI4vOTrfqDsVnP3DMC1BolGhGa0tozU74HKget_Zho8vnlqkNXDPDxa0

3. Covey, S. (2004). *Seven habits of highly effective people*. Salt Lake City, Utah: Franklin Covey Free Press.

4. Smith, W. (2022, February). No profession in the world has to create the system they work in as they go—except for teachers [Post]. LinkedIn. https://www.linkedin.com/in/waltersmith1/recent-activity/shares/

Bibliography

Ablin, J. [@JasonAblin]. (2022, May 7). We need a national center for teachers in their first five years of education. Fully funded. Run by master educators [Post].Twitter. https://twitter.com/search?q=We%20need%20a%20national%20center%20for%20teachers%20in%20their%20first%20five%20years%20of%20education.%20Fully%20funded.%20Run%20by%20master%20educators&src=typed_query&f=top

Anonymous blogger. (2015, February 28). *The copy machine deserves a beating. Wordpress.* https://drpezz.wordpress.com/2013/11/03/the-copy-machine-deserves-a-beating/

Anonymous graduate student (2020, May 20). In C. McQueen *The one-two punch of teacher-leadership*. National Institute for Excellence in Teaching. https://www.niet.org/newsroom/show/blog/one-two-punch-of-teacher-leadership-candice-mcqueen

Cahill, M. (2022, May 12). The four-day school week: Everything you wanted to know. *The Hungry Teacher Blog.* https://thehungryteacherblog.com/2018/03/the-four-day-school-week.html

Carver-Thomas, D., Burns, D., Leung, M., & Ondrasek, N. (2022, January 26). *Teacher shortages during the pandemic: How California districts are responding*. The Learning Policy Institute. https://learningpolicyinstitute.org/sites/default/files/product-files/Teacher_Shortages_During_Pandemic_REPORT.pdf

Cooban, A. (2022, August 1). *How the world's biggest four-day workweek trial run changed people's lives.* CNN Business. https://www.cnn.com/2022/08/01/business/4-day-work-week-uk-trial/index.html

Cooper, K. (2022, February). *Do our children deserve better?* Holistic Learning. https://holisticlearning.co.uk/do-our-children-deserve-better/

Costa, A., & Kallick, B. (2022). *What are habits of mind?* The Institute for Habits of Mind. https://www.habitsofmindinstitute.org/what-are-habits-of-mind/)

Covey, S. (2004). *Seven habits of highly effective people.* Salt Lake City, Utah: Franklin Covey Free Press.

Dayton, D. (2021, August 12). *What do Canadian teachers earn?* CHRON. https://work.chron.com/canadian-teachers-earn-13810.html

DeMallie, S. (2022, February). more time within their workday to do the things they need to do in order to be a better teacher [Post]. LinkedIn. https://www.linkedin.com/in/suzanne-demallie/recent-activity/

Dewey, J. (1907). *The school and society.* Chicago, Illinois: University of Chicago Press.

Edwards, T. [@tracyrenee70]. (2022, March 2). Twitter. Sat through a webinar on teacher resilience & was asked to share my thoughts. My answer: I don't want to [Tweet]. Twitter. https://twitter.com/tracyrenee70/status/1498812420239675392; https://stewweb.com/instructor-resiliency-isnt-whats-wanted-in-schooling-as-of-late/

Ernestus, S. [@DrErnestus]. (2021, September 5). I am, once again, asking people to stop using resilience as an individual trait (instead of a process or outcome) [Tweet]. Twitter. https://twitter.com/DrErnestus/status/1434694860783689734

Fischer, R. (2004). *The creation of Disneyland.* American Beat. http://www.plosin.com/beatbegins/projects/fischer.html

French, A. & Prendergast, L. (2022, May 31). Systems and structures for keeping your best teachers. *ASCD.* https://www.ascd.org/blogs/systems-and-structures-for-keeping-your-best-teachers

Fuchs, L. (2022, May 13). It would be uninterrupted. Too often the prep time is taken over by meetings, covering something, or other administrative tasks [Post]. LinkedIn. https://www.linkedin.com/in/lori-fuchs-m-ed-6644a3179/recent-activity/

Fullan, M. (2007, Summer). Change the terms for teacher learning. Thought Leader. *National Staff Development Council, 28*(3), 35–36. http://michaelfullan.ca/wp-content/uploads/2016/06/13396074650.pdf/

Gray, K. (2019, October 22). *Dear school administrators, please stop taking away teacher planning periods.* We are Teachers. https://www.weareteachers.com/i-need-my-planning-periods/

Haberlin, S. (2023). Want teacher to be happy? Let them be creative. *Education World.* https://www.educationworld.com/blog/want-teachers-be-happy-let-them-be-creative

Habits of Mind. (2022). *What are the Habits of Mind?* The Institute for Habits of Mind. https://www.habitsofmindinstitute.org/what-are-habits-of-mind/

Harris, B., Kolodner, M., & Morton, N. (2020, November 2). Rundown schools forced more students to go remote. *The Hechinger Report.* https://hechingerreport.org/rundown-schools-forced-more-students-to-go-remote

Harvard Graduate School of Education. (2022). *Multiple Intelligences.* Project Zero. http://www.pz.harvard.edu/projects/multiple-intelligences

Harvard Project Zero. (2022). *What is PZ?* Project Zero. http://www.pz.harvard.edu/who-we-are/about

Hudson, L. (2022, May 13). Teach Monday-Thursday, plan on Friday. Don't full planning day with useless PD or meetings. Teams meet if needed, not because [Post]. LinkedIn. https://www.linkedin.com/in/lmims/recent-activity/

Johnson, B. [@DrBradJohnson]. (2022, May 29). We can't expect teachers to work 60–70 hrs per week or more, but then tell them to self care. Maybe [Tweet]. Twitter. https://twitter.com/DrBradJohnson/status/1530957357735460866

Kamenetz, A. (2022, February 21). *More than half of teachers are looking for the exits, a poll says.* Mindshift. https://www.kqed.org/mindshift/59018/more-than-half-of-teachers-are-looking-for-the-exits-a-poll-says

Kelly, J. (2022, March 11). *Teachers are not to blame for their own burnout.* School Management Plus. https://www.schoolmanagementplus.com/heads-governors-school-leadership-governance/teachers-are-not-to-blame-for-their-own-burnout/

Kettering. C. F. (2023). Quotes in Goodreads. https://www.goodreads.com/quotes/887691-you-can-t-have-a-better-tomorrow-if-you-are-thinking

Kreidler, M. (2022, June 2). *California public schools are losing underpaid teachers at a steep rate.* Capital and Main. https://capitalandmain.com/california-public-schools-are-losing-underpaid-teachers-at-a-steep-rate

Laber-Warren, E. (2022, March 17). The 9-to-5 Schedule Should Be the Next Pillar of Work to Fall. *The New York Times.* https://www.nytimes.com/2022/03/17/opinion/work-flexibility-hours.html

Lave, J., & Wenger, E. (1991). *Situated learning: Legitimate peripheral participation.* Cambridge, England: Cambridge University Press.

Lawrence, M. (2020). *Testing 3-2-1: What Australian education can learn from Finland?* Melbourne VIC, Australia: Melbourne Books.

Learning Policy Institute. (2022, April 14). Teacher salaries: A key factor in recruitment and retention. https://learningpolicyinstitute.org/blog/teacher-salaries-key-factor-recruitment-and-retention

Lee, C. (2022, May 13). First there would be block time with 2 teachers, ed assistant and/or sp ed to determine the student schedule on [Post]. LinkedIn. https://www.linkedin.com/in/cap-lee-914831/recent-activity/

Leichtman, K. (2022, May 26). *How burned out are you? A scale for teachers.* Edutopia. https://www.edutopia.org/article/how-burned-out-are-you-scale-teachers

Mauriello, T. (2022, June 15). *Michigan House passes bill to pay student teachers for classroom work.* Bridge Michigan. https://www.bridgemi.com/talent-education/michigan-house-passes-bill-pay-student-teachers-classroom-work

McCabe, M. T. (2022, March). Honor them: Acknowledge the good things happening in their classroom, as well as their efforts outside the classroom (if they [Post]. LinkedIn. https://www.linkedin.com/in/maria-t-mccabe-75954a58/recent-activity/

McQueen, C. (2020, May 20). The one-two punch of teacher leadership. *National Institute for Excellence in Education.* https://www.niet.org/newsroom/show/blog/one-two-punch-of-teacher-leadership-candice-mcqueen

Mielke, C. (2019). *The burnout cure: Learning to love teaching again.* Alexandria, Virginia: ASCD.

Nathan, L. (2014, July 25). We have allowed the state to declare war on schools and teachers. *Boston Review.* https://bostonreview.net/forum_response/linda-nathan-habits-mind/

National Association of Colleges and Employers. (2020, September 4). *Average salary for class of 2019 up almost 6 percent over class of 2018's.* https://www.naceweb.org/job-market/compensation/average-salary-for-class-of-2019-up-almost-6-percent-over-class-of-2018s/

Neretlis, J. (2022, February). We've made our school purposefully joyful. It means having displays, art, and areas that lets children be imaginative in their [Post]. LinkedIn. https://www.linkedin.com/in/john-neretlis-mba-970385b8/recent-activity/

Nordengren, C. (2016). Teaching new dogs new tricks: Teacher leadership in the performance assessment for California teachers (PACT). *Issues in Teacher Education, 25*(1), 91–106.

Nordengren, C. (2016). Educators want opportunities for teacher-leadership, too. *ASCD.* https://www.ascd.org/el/articles/new-educators-want-opportunities-for-teacher-leadership-too

OECD. (2018). *Teachers' salaries (indicator).* https://data.oecd.org/eduresource/teachers-alaries.htm

Owen, R. (2022, April 21). Can we make real, transformative change in education? *Greater Good Magazine.* https://greatergood.berkeley.edu/article/item/can_we_make_real_transformative_change_in_education?fbclid=IwAR1hI4vOTrfqDsVnP3DMC1BolGhGa0tozU74HKget_Zho8vnlqkNXDPDxa0

Paterson, C. (2022, March 29). *Who is going to teach the kids?* Getting Smart. https://www.gettingsmart.com/2022/03/29/who-is-going-to-teach-the-kids/

Patrick, S. K. & Carver-Thomas, D. (2022, April 14). Teacher salaries: A key factor in recruitment and retention. *Learning Policy Institute.* https://learningpolicyinstitute.org/blog/teacher-salaries-key-factor-recruitment-and-retention

PA Media. (2022, April 11). 44% of teachers in England plan to quit within five years. *The Guardian.* https://www.theguardian.com/education/2022/apr/11/teachers-england-plan-to-quit-workloads-stress-trust

Pillow, A. (2021, July 26). *We all hate professional development but some of yall need it.* Ed post. https://www.edpost.com/stories/we-all-hate-professional-development-but-some-of-yall-need-it

Rablin, T. [@Mr_Rablin]. (2022, May 30). Every single school should be working to figure out how to double plan time for teachers. The US requires more [Tweet]. Twitter. https://twitter.com/Mr_Rablin/status/1531386199314616321

Ramirez, L. (2020, March 5). *Why teachers are saying goodbye* [Post]. LinkedIn. https://www.linkedin.com/pulse/why-teachers-saying-goodbye-lexi-evans/?trackingId=HBk6xADMU0JL%2BVj2SBH2gA%3D%3D

Rath, T. (2007). *Strengthfinder 2.0.* New York: Gallup Press.

Reeves, D. B. (2016). *From leading to succeeding: The seven elements of effective leadership in education.* Bloomington, Indiana: Solution Tree Press.

Reeves, D. B. (2018, May 1). Seven keys to restoring the teacher pipeline. *ASCD.* https://www.ascd.org/el/articles/seven-keys-to-restoring-the-teacher-pipeline

Reeves, D. B. (2019, July 14). *Too many standards–too little time.* Creative Leadership Solutions. https://www.creativeleadership.net/blog/too-many-standards-too-little-time

Rimes, B. (2014, December 5). *Technology will not revolutionize education.* The Tech Savvy Educator. https://www.techsavvyed.net/archives/3754

Robinson, D. (2022, March). Aspirational school leaders tend to use their teaching staff to try out new ideas and set new goals for the [Post]. LinkedIn. https://www.linkedin.com/in/daniel-robinson-teacher/recent-activity/

Sadaka, G. (2022, February 12). !Mental Health resources which include professional development! [Post]. LinkedIn. https://www.linkedin.com/in/ghadasadaka/recent-activity/

Sahlberg, P. (2022, June 7). *New Education Minister Jason Clare can fix the teacher shortage crisis—but not with Labor's election plan.* The Conversation. https://theconversation.com/new-education-minister-jason-clare-can-fix-the-teacher-shortage-crisis-but-not-with-labors-election-plan-184321

Smith, B. J. (2011). ELA Curriculum. Jalen Rose Leadership Academy (JRLA). Detroit, Michigan.

Smith, B. J. (2013). WEDJ School Math Essential Skills and Understandings (Grades Pre-K to 2nd Grade). WEDJ School Curriculum. Washington, DC.

Smith, B. J. (2013). WEDJ School Math Essential Skills and Understandings (3rd to 5th Grade). WEDJ School Curriculum. Washington, DC.

Smith, B. J. (2013). WEDJ School Math Essential Skills and Understandings (6th to 8th Grade). WEDJ School Curriculum. Washington, DC.

Smith, B. J. (2021). *How much does a great school cost? School economies and school values*. Lanham, MD: Rowman & Littlefield.

Smith, B. J. (2023). *Assessment tools and systems: Meaningful Feedback Approaches to Promote Critical and Creative Thinking*. Lanham, MD: Rowman & Littlefield.

Smith, W. (2022, February). No profession in the world has to create the system they work in as they go - except for teachers [Post]. LinkedIn. https://www.linkedin.com/in/waltersmith1/recent-activity/shares/

Soojung-Kim Pang, A. (2018). *Rest: Why you get more done when you work less*. New York: Basic Books.

Statistics Canada. (2020). *Table C.3.1. Annual statutory teachers' salaries in public institutions, by level of education taught and teaching experience, Canadian dollars, Canada, provinces and territories, 2018/2019*. https://www150.statcan.gc.ca/n1/pub/81-604-x/2020001/tbl/tblc3.1-eng.htm

Stieber, D. (2022, February 14). *America's teachers aren't burned out. We are demoralized*. EdSurge. https://www.edsurge.com/news/2022-02-14-america-s-teachers-aren-t-burned-out-we-are-demoralized

Stroud, G. (2018). *Teacher*. In C. Paterson's *Who is going to teach the kids?* (2022, March 29). Getting Smart. https://www.gettingsmart.com/2022/03/29/who-is-going-to-teach-the-kids/

Syed, S. [@MDinWaiting]. (2021, September 3). Did it hurt? When you poured out your trauma to get into med school and were praised for being resilient [Tweet]. Twitter. https://twitter.com/MDinWaiting/status/1433955039899369474

Tamez-Robledo, N. (2022, June 22). *Can four-day school weeks keep teachers from leaving?* EdSurge. https://www.edsurge.com/news/2022-06-22-can-four-day-school-weeks-keep-teachers-from-leaving

That ELA Teacher [@saneELAteacher]. (2022, April 26). I've said it before and I'll say it again: it blows my mind how manageable a class is when I [Post]. Twitter. https://twitter.com/saneELAteacher/status/1518971342229590017

The Alberta Teachers' Federation. (2023). *PD activities for Professional Growth*. https://www.teachers.ab.ca/For%20Members/ProfessionalGrowth/Section%203/Pages/Professional%20Development%20Activities%20for%20Teachers.aspx

The Guardian (April 11, 2022). *44% of teachers in England plan to quit within five years*. https://www.theguardian.com/education/2022/apr/11/teachers-england-plan-to-quit-workloads-stress-trust

Todd, A. (2021, September). How to build leadership capabilities that'll keep your employees engaged. *Udemy*. https://blog.udemy.com/leadership-training-topics/

Valenzuela, J. (2022, March 3). *Boosting critical thinking across the curriculum*. Edutopia. George Lucas Foundation. https://www.edutopia.org/article/boosting-critical-thinking-across-curriculum

Vygotsky, L. S. (1978). *Mind in society: The development of higher psychological processes*. Cambridge, Massachusetts: Harvard University Press.

Walker, T. (2015, August 26). Want to reduce the teacher shortage? Treat teachers like professionals (An interview with Richard Ingersoll). *NEA Today*. https://www.nea.org/advocating-for-change/new-from-nea/want-reduce-teacher-shortage-treat-teachers-professionals

Zinn, L. F. (1997). *Supports and barriers to teacher leadership: Reports of teacher leaders*. AERA. https://lsc-net.terc.edu/do/paper/8120/show/page-3/use_set-ldrshp.html

About the Author

Barbara J. Smith is an educator and researcher who is committed to a lifelong learning quest to improve the conditions for schooling at home and globally. Throughout Smith's career, she has taken on many different roles in many different schools. She began teaching middle school for the Waterloo County Board of Education in 1980. Smith will say her students taught her how to adapt her teaching to not just meet their needs but to support them to become student leaders who collectively made all sorts of creative and authentic things happen in schools. Barbara's move to high school had her working in four departments (math, English, science, and physical and health education) in addition to coaching the school gymnastics team and dance company. In the summers Barbara often brought her student leaders to be co-teachers when she taught additional qualification courses at the University of Toronto.

After five years, Smith applied for a health consultant position, a district-level support role for 115 elementary and 15 high schools. Realizing the importance of moving beyond health knowledge to attitudes and behaviors, Barbara researched and compared health knowledge of Waterloo students with other students in Canada who participated in a nationwide assessment. She was well aware that, regardless of the knowledge scores, students needed classroom experiences that supported healthy choices and habits. Smith worked with a local high school and 12 nearby elementary schools to pilot a peer-teaching program where grade 10 students prepared and presented lessons on smoke-free living. The Canadian Lung Association supported the efforts by providing many free resources. The high school students, who became peer teachers, all journaled about how much they enjoyed the opportunity. Many who were smokers quit. Captivated by the attitudinal and behavioral shift, Barbara studied about peer teaching for years, culminating her search in her PhD thesis, which highlighted the transformation of grade 4 students teaching younger classes at Queenston Public School in the Peel Board of Education near Toronto.

Smith moved back and forth between teacher educator roles at the three Canadian universities and being in classrooms where she could examine the teaching and learning context firsthand. Students of all ages have been her mentors. Her students in the Indigenous teacher education program at the University of Saskatchewan coordinated an incredible health fair, breathing life into community resources and making the messages relevant for their context. Having an opportunity to blend current research with practice in such teacher preparation roles provided a wake-up call for Smith, as she discovered an alarming gap between teaching theory and practice. In between her work in Saskatchewan, McGill University in Montreal, and the University of Toronto, Barbara taught grade 1, music, special education and designed new inquiry-based courses in grades 3 through 8 in public, independent, international, and charter schools.

As a curriculum coordinator at the International School of Brussels (ISB) followed by the VP of academics role at the Sterling Hall School for boys in Toronto, Smith worked with staff and students to introduce a number of teaching and learning innovations. Students at ISB designed a peer-teaching course, which was presented at a European Project Zero Conference. Teachers at Sterling Hall designed a dozen new elective courses, including journalism, robotics, coaching, novel writing, yearbook design, and musicians in residency. Smith edited and supported many staff members who contributed chapters in a book called: *Ask Me about My Action Research*. Grade 3, 4, and 5 students presented about their experiences in the Sterling Has Action Research Kids (SHARK) inquiry program at the International Boys Schools Coalition Conferences.

Smith recognized that changing the landscape of schools would involve becoming a principal and opening new schools. As part of the founding team at the Jalen Rose Leadership Academy high school, she coordinated curriculum guides, resource material, professional development, and the hiring of the first team of educators. The distinct schedule enabled students to sleep in on Wednesday mornings, giving teachers a chance for extended professional learning. In the afternoon the students were bused to a senior's home, where they wrote and published their buddy's biography. Making memories was a high priority. Giving many young people from disadvantaged families an opportunity to research primary sources, write for a purpose, and learn from elders provided deep learning experiences. At this time Smith was stunned by the naïve assumption held by many stakeholders that the measure of school greatness was summed up by average test scores, which ranked schools against each other. Widespread understandings of mastery and other grounded practices did not seem to be commonplace in this educational context.

Similarly, the wrath of simplifying schools to one-page dashboards was ever present in Washington, DC, as students in all public and charter schools were tested beginning in grade 3. For Smith it felt like the *Twilight Zone*, light years away from the grounded messages coming from experts supporting approaches such as Harvard *Project Zero* (PZ), Habits of Mind, and Growth Mindsets. Concerned about the dated doctrines that seemed to permeate charter schools, Smith invested in professional learning to the tune of $35,000 to send 12 teachers to Boston to take part in a week-long PZ professional learning. If teachers need to help their students transform, schools need teacher leadership teams that understand the value of change and school improvement.

Following her principal and executive director role at the William Doar School for the Performing Arts, Barbara became the founding principal of Middleburg Charter School in Virginia. The opportunity to implement innovative programming was refreshing, as parents on the board had done their homework, learning about integrated curriculum and committing to establishing a Leonardo da Vinci–inspired school.

Upon return to Canada, Smith was part of a team that opened a school focused on entrepreneurship and environmentalism. The two-room schoolhouse featured an imagination center—where social studies and English language arts (ELA) were integrated—as well as an innovation center—where math and science was taught. Students in this school spent at least one day a week in the community, learning about many fields of work.

Barbara's most recent principal role was in an independent school in Toronto where students focused on a global education, which included learning the six official languages of the United Nations, as well as a Model UN course integrated into social studies. All students had several years of chess, coding, robotics, and debating as part of their regular course of study. The goal of preparing students for everything was ever present within this globally minded school.

Apart from exploring innovative and creative ideas to engage staff and students, the common thread through her 40 years as an educator was her desire to teach in every context and in every role. Smith believes all school administrators, deans, department of education officials, academic leaders, academic coaches, librarians, guidance counsellors, special education teachers, and ELL teachers should have dedicated time in regular classrooms to teach and keep current with changing teaching and learning cultures. In that way teachers and school leaders can be open to change and brave enough to invest in practices that can lead to significant school improvement.

PRAISE FOR *TEACHER SHORTAGES AND THE CHALLENGE OF RETENTION*

"*Teacher Shortages and the Challenge of Retention* is a must read for principals and school leaders. Not only does it concisely group the challenges needing immediate addressing in schools, it provides thought-provoking ideas, stemming from real scenarios where success has occurred. Smith is still an educator through and through, evidenced by her 'Challenge Chats' section at chapter conclusion, wanting readers to engage in rigorous dialogue, guiding them to solutions in their context."

—Liam Exelby, founder and director, YXL Institute, Australia

"*Teacher Shortages and the Challenge of Retention* is as real as it gets. Barbara Smith expertly unpacks the causes, conditions, and barriers that keep the profession in a state of decline. The good news is she also provides a roadmap for real, practical, and sustainable solutions. This book is a must read for every education organization, family, and community."

—Kate Anderson Foley, PhD, chief executive officer, the Education Policy & Practice Group, Lakewood, Ohio (US)

"*Teacher Shortages and the Challenge of Retention* successfully communicates a vision where schools become a culture of continuous improvement by articulating the role of teachers as leaders in the instructional change process in a way that honors and recognizes their professionalism. It does so by redefining the evaluation process as an 'instructional' partnership where both the teacher and the supervising administrator recognize that both have equal responsibility in the successful implementation of change. The book also spells out the critical role of a relationship with parents and the school community that positions the school as an institution that should reflect the values of the community it serves. I recommend this excellent resource for any wanting to understand how to change schools for the better while respecting the hard work of teachers and others who on an everyday basis serve the educational need of the students in the communities across our nation."

—Hardy Murphy, PhD, (former school superintendent), clinical professor of Educational Leadership and Policy Studies, Indiana University (US)

"In this book, Barbara loads our toolbox full of useful tools to engage teachers and education professionals. Thinking longer term, one could easily take four or five of her chapters/tactics and craft an effective 5-year strategic HR plan for a school or board. The results would benefit students (our main stakeholder) as much as teachers. Administrators, it's time to be leaders!"

—John Neretlis, director, Brick Labs Inc., Toronto, Canada

"In this vitally important book, Barbara Smith cuts to the heart of the challenges facing education: time, resources, and respect. Every citizen has a stake in improving education, and our collective failure to heed Smith's warnings will impose costs on all of us, whether or not we have children in school. This is a book not only for teachers and school leaders but for policymakers and the citizens who elect them."

—Douglas Reeves, author, Fearless Schools, CEO, Creative Leadership Solutions, Boston, MA (US)

"What makes Barbara Smith worth paying close attention to is the breadth of her educational experience and the consequent depth of her analysis. She has a knack for getting directly to the heart of the matter, and this latest book is no exception. A fresh and insightful response to a challenge that must be overcome. Five stars!"

—Ted Spear, PhD, author of *Education Reimagined: The Schools Our Children Need*, Vancouver, Canada

"Barbara Smith has a microscopic and telescopic view of educational systems. This resource provides a rich reflection on the challenges of engaging, encouraging, and empowering those who choose to be part of the wonderful world of teaching. This book is an important, authentic document that provides information and invitations and insights for those on their journeys as educators—yesterday, today and tomorrow."

—Larry Swartz, instructor, Ontario Institute for Studies in Education, University of Toronto (OISE, UofT), Canada

"With the ongoing crisis in our schools only being exacerbated by the COVID pandemic, it is time for a serious rethink. Barbara explores each of the main key areas in an insightful and honest assessment and then leaves the reader with key questions to enable 'Challenging Chats' amongst staff. Fantastic resource for teachers and school executives who are ready to start questioning the status quo and transition to a better future for everyone."

—Dr. Mark Williams, professor of Cognitive Neuroscience, Macquarie University, Sydney, Australia

"Dr. Barbara Smith clearly articulates the factors and challenges to addressing teacher retention in our schools. Many of the challenges highlighted in *Teacher Shortage and Challenges of Retention* are familiar to educators, but the practical and holistic approach is refreshing. Everything from teacher resources to parent relationships is covered. A thought-provoking and strategic book all school leaders should read."

—Adam Weber, CEO of Truwell

www.ingramcontent.com/pod-product-compliance
Lightning Source LLC
Chambersburg PA
CBHW032028230426
43671CB00005B/236